GW00586474

THE GUNN REPORT
AND SHOWREEL OF THE YEAR

2005

Sponsored by
Procter & Gamble
P&G

Edited by Donald Gunn

Presented in association with
FlaxmanWilkie

The Gunn Report and Showreel of The Year 2005

Devised and edited by Donald Gunn
Published by FlaxmanWilkie

Research & Compilation	Emma Wilkie
Tabulation	Emma Wilkie
	Donald Gunn
Assistants	Sophie Gunn
	Felix Wilkie
Synopses	Donald Gunn
	Drew Wehrle
Production Director & Publisher	Mike Wilkie

Very special thanks to Patty Alvey, Rafa Anton, Michael Conrad & Roger Kennedy

FlaxmanWilkie
Reed Hall, Ipswich Road, Holbrook,
Suffolk, IP9 2QR, England
Tel: +44 (0)1473 326 999
Fax: +44 (0)1473 328 422
Email: mike@gunnreport.com
Web: www.gunnreport.com

Production Design by Poulsen Selleck
poulsenselleck.com

Printed and Bound by Butler and Tanner

ISBN-10: 0-9551646-0-5
ISBN-13: 978-0-9551646-0-6

Donald   Emma   Mike

Contents

The Gunn Report 2005 Summary

i Commercial or TV/Cinema Campaign of the Year:

Honda Diesel • Grrr   Wieden+Kennedy (London)

Runners up: adidas • Laila - 180 Amsterdam (180/TBWA) &
Canadian Short Film Festival • Good Cop. Bad Cop / Special FX / Love Story & campaign - Taxi (Toronto)

ii Print Ad or Campaign of the Year:

Tamiya Model Kits Shop • Light Bulb / Frog / Watermelon   Creative Juice/G1 (Bangkok)

Runners up: Anglican Welfare Council • Churchill / Chaplin / Newton - O&M Singapore &
Volkswagen Polo • King Kong - DDB London

iii Country of the Year:

USA

Runners up: Great Britain & France

iv Advertiser of the Year:

Volkswagen

Runners up: adidas & Sony

v Production Company of the Year:

Phenomena (Bangkok)

Runners up: @radical.media (London, Paris, Berlin, Sydney, New York) &
Biscuit Filmworks (Los Angeles); Nexus (London)

vi Director of the Year:

Thanonchai Sornsrivichai (Thailand)

Runners up: Adam Foulkes/Alan Smith (Great Britain); Noam Murro (USA)

vii Agency of the Year:

AlmapBBDO (Sao Paulo)

Runners up: TBWA\Paris & Dentsu (Tokyo & Osaka)

viii Agency Network of the Year:

TBWA Worldwide

Runners up: BBDO Worldwide & DDB Worldwide

Foreword

I honestly hope this is the low point of the book.

In fact, I think there's a good chance you'll never read all the way to the end of this foreword. That's understandable.

The ads and insights that follow are by far more interesting and exciting than a corporate sponsor's discussion on how your collective creativity is inspiring and energizing one of the world's largest advertisers.

How our very communication model is being reinvented -– even as you thumb through the tables and watch your favorite spots over and over again.

How Procter & Gamble's belief in creative is matched and surpassed only by our faith in consumers who show us, time and again, that "creative" and "effective" advertising can be, and often is, one in the same.

Yes, there's a good chance that instead of investing the time to read all the way to this point, you've already gone on to view the best of the best – to be inspired, to applaud brilliance, to be jealous, to gloat, to light a fire under somebody or to set those consumer hearts on fire yet again.

But, to those tenacious few who've read all the way to this point, I have only one thing to say: what are you waiting for?

All the best,

Jim Stengel
Global Marketing Officer
Procter & Gamble

P&G

Industry News.

Accounts in Review.

Guest Columnists.

The Top Shops.

The Best Creatives.

E-mail News Alerts.

Analysis/Perspective.

In print and online.

We've got you covered.

www.adweek.com

Wright Ferguson, Jr., Publisher
wferguson@adweek.com

THE GUNN REP●RT

Commentary & League Tables

2005

The annual worldwide league
tables for the advertising industry

Commercials, Print Ads,
Countries, Advertisers,
Production Co's, Directors,
Agencies and Agency Networks

MILLIONS OF HIS T-SHIRTS WERE SOLD, HE WAS AGAINST CAPITALISM.

LATIN AMERICA IS UNPREDICTABLE. THAT MAKES US THINK DIFFERENT.

Introducing The Gunn Report 2005

Welcome to the seventh annual edition of The Gunn Report – The Gunn Report 2005.

Since 1999, every November, The Gunn Report has combined the winners' lists from all of the world's most important award contests (top 34 shows TV, top 21 Print for 2005) thus to establish the annual, worldwide "league tables" for the advertising industry.

2005 *highlights* of The Report itself include the following:

Commercials league table won by the biggest points margin ever – by Honda "Grrr", of course, Grand Prix or Best of Show at 7 major shows. In the Print Ads table, 1st and 2nd places go to Asia – to Thailand and Singapore. France and Germany consolidate on their surge up the Countries table, at the expense of "the Latin Bloc".

In the Advertisers table, exactly the same top 5 as in 2004, with Volkswagen notching up an amazing 6th win in 7 years. Thailand take top place not just in the Productions Companies table for 2005, but also in the Directors table.

In the case of Agencies, 4 of the Top 5 in 2005 were previous winners and one of these won again to become the first ever 2-time winner of Table 7. Finally, in Agency Networks, a first time winner of the table, moving up from 2nd place in both 2003 and 2004, and scoring the highest points total ever.

On the general Gunn Report news front, the leading stories are

i Format: our new format – The Book (which replaced the box in 2004 and which you have in your hands right now) – has been a big success. Sales up nearly 400%, despite us having sent out the first 1000 (nearly) copies of the 2004 Book free to the year's top winners.

We continue this policy for 2005, though not on quite such a reckless scale. Copies will go out free, with our compliments and congratulations, to the 100 most awarded agencies in the world – ECD and CEO in each – as well as to all of the Advertisers and Production Companies and Directors in tables 4, 5 and 6, as well as to all of the world's leading advertising and marketing schools and colleges. Re which, your 2005 Book contains one new section – Student - which showcases the "Best of Show" work from the leading student advertising contests of the last 12 months.

ii. Sponsorship: Procter & Gamble continue as overall sponsor of The Gunn Report, and we are very proud of this. We count ourselves truly fortunate that P&G take a real interest in our work and contribute very useful ideas in addition to valuable funding.

iii. The Gunn Report for Media: also sponsored by Procter & Gamble, and using the same methodology as this Report, audits and measures the results of nearly 40 media contests and festivals round the world. The Media Report is implemented by managing editor, Isabelle Musnik. The first edition came out in October 2004, the second in October 2005. The written Report is made available to media networks and agencies all around the world – as well as to the trade and business press. For 2006, a Book and DVD, presenting not just the Report and Tables but also showcasing a lavish range of the winning work, is planned.

iv. The Gunn Report Library@BEAM.tv: The world's smallest on-line commercials library. Only 100 selections (commercials and campaigns) per year ever go in (starting with those that have made The Showreel of The Year from 1999 to 2005). Plus an average of 60 selections per year from 1998 – 1990; 40 selections per year from 1989 – 1980; plus the 250 or so best from the 70's and 60's – chosen on the same basis, the world's most awarded and applauded every year. The Gunn Report Library@BEAM.tv has been up and running as of October 1st 2005.

And now, for all the rankings, tables and winners for the year 2005, please read on…

Think it. Disrupt it. Connect it.

TBWA

1 • Commercials

Table One on page 36 presents the 50 most awarded commercials and campaigns in the world in 2005.

The USA with 10 in the top 50 and Great Britain with 9 are the two most represented countries, just as last year. France came next with 6 in the top 50; Argentina and Canada each had 4; Germany and Thailand each had 3; Brazil, Japan and The Netherlands each had 2; while Italy, Mexico, Peru, South Africa and Sweden had 1 commercial or campaign apiece in the 2005 Table.

An interesting feature this year is that no fewer than 15 of the 50 making the table had been featured on The Gunn Report's Showreel of The Year 2004, but then kept on winning in 2005. These included the work that was 2nd, 3rd and 4th equal placed in the Table. 15 from the previous year's Showreel of The Year is more than ever previously, comparing to 8 in 2004 and 9 in 2003. I suppose it suggests we're doing our job quite well: spotting the best stuff early on in its award winning career and not making you wait a year for it.

Great Britain scooped up no less than 6 of the Top Ten places in 2005, including rankings 10th to 7th. 10th most awarded commercial or campaign in the world in 2005 was Citroen C4 "Carbot" (Euro RSCG, London). 9th was Stella Artois "Pilot" (Lowe, London). 8th was the new pool in the Orange "Don't Ruin The Movie" campaign (Mother, London). 7th came the highly admired NSPCC "Ventriloquist" commercial from Saatchi & Saatchi, London. 6th place in the table in 2005 went to Germany with Volkswagen Golf DSG "Kids on Steps" from DDB Germany.

4th equal places, they both had 14 ad points, were taken by two of the all-star selections on our 2004 Showreel: Lynx 24-7 "Getting Dressed" and Peugeot 407 "Toys". "Getting Dressed" (from Bartle Bogle Hegarty, London and production company: Small Family Business – director: Ringan Ledwidge) debuted at Cannes last year and then won Grand Prix in Ireland (Shark Awards) before adding further honours this year at D&AD, British Television and the Andys.

"Toys" (BETC Euro RSCG, Paris and Wanda Productions, Paris – director: Philippe André) also took Gold at Cannes 2004, before piling up 2005 ad points at Eurobest, Andys, Clios and ADC*E, etc.

With one point higher, 15 ad points, 3rd place in the 2005 Table went to the Canadian Short Film Festival campaign (Taxi, Toronto and Untitled, Toronto – director: Tim Godsall) – another with an ardent audience approval factor anywhere I showed a reel. Got its Cannes Gold in 2004, then was in the honours at One Show, Clios, New York Art Directors Club and Bessies (of course) among the 2005 shows.

adidas "Laila" (180 Amsterdam and Park Pictures, New York – director: Lance Acord) notched up 4 points more – 19 ad points in total in 2005 – to come in second in our Table. Winning Cannes Gold (in conjunction with "Long Run") in 2004, this predecessor of this year's brilliant pool – "Nadia"/"Jesse"/"Haile" (see 27th place) - scored again for 2005 in all 3 pan-European shows, the German and Dutch ADC's, and Andy's, NYADC, One Show and more.

Then we have a huge jump – easily the biggest ever jump between runner-up and winner in Table One of The Gunn Report – from 19 to 35 points! These 35 points were amassed, of course, by Honda "Grrr". This tour de force from Wieden+Kennedy, London and Nexus Productions, London – directors: Adam Foulkes and Alan Smith – not to put too fine a point on it was a shoo-in for the Grand Prix (or equivalent) just about everywhere it was entered – Epica (first of all), then British Television, Andys, Clios, One Show, Cannes and Sharks to name but seven.

No commercial in the 7-year-history of The Gunn Report has won Table One by such an overwhelming margin. And no commercial in history, since Apple "1984" in 1984, has been such an odds-on favourite to take the Cannes Grand Prix – as well as that being virtually everyone's wish. This commercial goes direct (it doesn't have to pass "Go") to The Gunn Report's reel of "The 100 Best Commercials of All-Time". Warmest congratulations to all who had a hand in this truly wonderful achievement.

We're as similar as we're different.

 Brother" in Vietnam, "friend of the people" in China and "wood of the poor" in India. These are just a few of the many names for bamboo, a grass so practical yet so sumptuously intertwined with the roots of Asian culture.

As far back as 2 BC, the Chinese recorded their legends and history on bamboo strips strung together with silk thread. Later, its pulp led to the invention of paper upon which centuries of paintings and poems were captured.

Today, bamboo's practical uses are endless. From the Philippines to Malaysia, this giant grass provides materials to build entire houses. Literally everything can be built from bamboo - roofs, walls, doors, floors, beds, tables and chairs. Even musical instruments, kites, rafts, fishing traps and baskets can be crafted out of this manufacturing marvel.

So incredibly versatile, bamboo can even be cooked and eaten. From Bangkok to Bombay, bamboo shoots are a familiar feature in many types of curry. In Japan,

the tender young shoots are a seasonal delicacy. The shoots are picked at the first signs of spring and everyone looks forward to the vegetarian specialty, *takenoko gohan*, a delicate melody of bamboo and rice.

Tuck into a bit of bamboo and you may also be warding off cancer and kidney disease. Bamboo has been used as a stimulant, aromatic and tonic in China, and in India, it is even believed to have aphrodisiac qualities.

All over Asia, bamboo is an integral part of life – from handicrafts to houses and fishing rods to fences. But amidst all its practicalities, bamboo is also aesthetically charming, symbolising the many different faces of Asia. Faces that we, at Dentsu, have grown to know so well.

At Dentsu, we understand the similarities that make Asian consumers different, as well as the differences that make us similar.

You might say, we've gone bamboo.

dentsu
BORN IN ASIA

1 • **Commercials** *cont.*

The chart below shows how the Top 10 totally new commercials and campaigns of 2005
(it doesn't include the "2004 continueds") fared at the Top 4 international shows:

	Cannes	Clio	One Show	D&AD
Honda Diesel "Grrr"	GP. JA	GC.G	BoS.G	2G/6S
VW Golf DSG "Kids on Steps"	B	S	S.B	n/w
NSPCC "Ventriloquist"	G	G	B	n
Citroen C4 "Carbot"	B	2G	n/w	S
VH1 TV "Parents Day" & campaign	S	B	G	n/e
Sony Playstation 2 "Athletes"/"Golfers" etc	G	G	S	book (6)
Mercedes "Sounds of Summer"	G	2S	book	book (3)
Ford Ranger Truck "King Kong"	G	B	n/e	n/e
INPES/Passive Smoking "Marie"	S	B	n/w	n/w
adidas "Unstoppable"	G	2G	G	n/w

(GP=Grand Prix / JA=Journalists Award / GC = Grand Clio / BoS = Best of Show / G=Gold / S=Silver / B=Bronze /
n=nomination / book=in book / n/w=entered, but didn't win / n/e=not entered)

So only "Grrr" of the above was a "metal" winner at all 4 shows: and only "Grrr" achieved the coveted Grand Slam:
Gold (or better) at Cannes, Gold (or better) at Clio, Gold (or better) at One Show, Silver (or better) at D&AD – *(and in
fact achieved "or better" in all 4 cases).*

We end this section, as we've done in previous years, with a listing – "The Most Promising Latecomers".
These are commercials or campaigns which debut towards the end of the award shows year, and so don't appear
in the Top 50 Table that year, but seem destined to become serial winners in the year ahead.

Nominations for the 6 Most Promising Latecomers of 2005 would be:
1). Aides Awareness "Vibrators" (France); 2). Viagra "Golf"/"Office"/"Coach" (Canada);
3). Rexona For Men "Stunt City" (Great Britain); 4). Levi's 501 With Anti-Fit "Midsummer" (Great Britain);
5.) Axe Body Spray "Residue" (USA); 6). Olympus Camera "Red-Eyed Boy"/"Cropped Dogs" etc (The Netherlands).

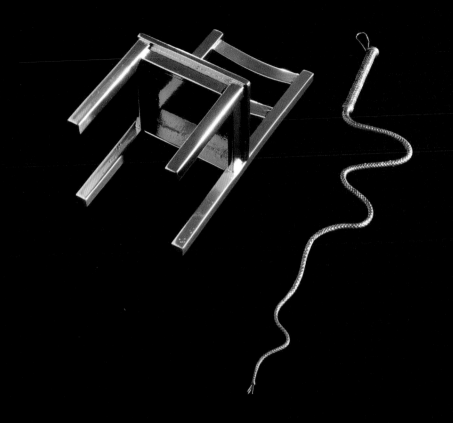

DDB. More awards at Cannes 2005 than any other network.

2 • Print Ads

Table Two presents the 50 most awarded print ads or campaigns in the world in 2005. Thirty two of these are campaigns as opposed to single ads: the other way round from TV, where thirty five out of the top 50 were single commercials and fifteen were campaigns.

Twenty one markets in total have made it into the Table, with the three most represented being Germany (7 ads and campaigns, 4 of which in top 20), Great Britain (7) and France (6). These were exactly the same three most represented markets as last year, when Germany, Great Britain and France took 6 places each.

Thailand with 4 ads and campaigns was the fourth most awarded country, followed by Brazil and Singapore 3 places each and Argentina, Australia, Mexico, Spain and the USA with 2 apiece. And Austria, Belgium, Canada, China, Czech Republic, Japan, Malaysia, Portugal, South Africa and the United Arab Emirates all had one in the Table.

The UAE is a notable newcomer to Table Two – and due to a truly outstanding ad. Sony Wega Engine TV "Paper Clip" from Tonic Communications in Dubai won Gold both at Cannes and the One Show.

It took 12 points in 2005 to get in the top 10 (11 pointers made it last year). Rankings 10th to 6th were claimed by 10th: the Weru Noise Protection Windows campaign (Scholz & Friends, Berlin); 9th: Time Magazine "Pendulum" (Fallon, New York); 8th: Pizza Hut Delivery campaign (BBDO, Singapore); 7th: adidas "Impossible Sprint" (TBWA\Japan); and in 6th place – The Economist "Light Bulb" (Abbott Mead Vickers.BBDO, London).

In 5th place in the world in 2005, on 15 ad points, came the highly admired "Flags" campaign for Grande Reportagem Magazine from Foote Cone & Belding in Lisbon, which took the Grand Prix both at FIAP and at ADC*E as well as Gold at Cannes and Gold at the One Show.

In 4th place, on 16 points, was the Bisley Office Furniture "Perfectly Organised" campaign from Kolle Rebbe Werbeagentur in Hamburg. Its many wins included One Show Gold and D&AD Silver. (Like Weru – see above – this advertiser followed up a top five ranking in our 2004 table, but with all new subjects).

Volkswagen Polo "King Kong" from DDB London came in 3rd in 2005 with 17 ad points – a winner at seven different shows in total – and a great sequel to 2004's table-topping ad: VW Polo "Cops".

Two points higher (19 ad points) – The Anglican Welfare Council campaign – "Churchill"/"Hitler"/"Newton", from Ogilvy & Mather in Singapore, was the second most awarded Print Ad or campaign in the world in 2005. It cleaned up in both the pan-Asian shows – Adfest and Media – as well as taking high honours at Cannes (Gold & Silver), One Show (Gold) and Clio.

With one point higher (20 ad points), to be the winner of Table Two in 2005, as the most awarded Print Ad or campaign in the world for the year, came Tamiya Model Kits Shop – "Light Bulb"/"Frog"/"Watermelon" – from Creative Juice/GI in Bangkok: Best of Print at Adfest and further prominent wins at Cannes, One Show, Clio and Media were among its formidable tally of honours.

At this point I will permit myself a little comment on the nature of the Advertisers taking some of the top places in our Table. While Fallon (then Fallon McElligott Rice) first became famous in the USA in the mid-80's by virtue of ads for barber shops in Minneapollis and the church around the corner, it has to be even more of an achievement to create and sell highly creative work to mainstream, big budget Clients. Maybe Jury Presidents at major shows should consider factoring in a modest "degree of difficulty" component based on the nature of Advertisers in contention and affecting the colour of metal awarded.

That said, both of our top two campaigns of 2005 are based on high quality original thinking and both are absolutely beautifully crafted and I'm sure we all want to celebrate them without reservation.

Finally, as explained in the last section, our "Most Promising Latecomer" nominations for Print from the year 2005 are as follows: 1) EMI Music Piracy Awareness campaign (France); 2) Wonderbra "Whiteboard" (Malaysia); 3) Axe Shower Gel campaign "Grip Pods"/"Mirror"/"Towels" (USA); 4) Lego "Street Building" (Chile); 5) the Kleenex Tissues campaign "Stuart"/"John"/"Morrell" (Brazil); 6) Pedigree Dog Biscuits "Forest"/"Lady" (France).

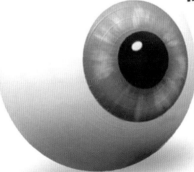

3 • Countries

See Table Three (on page 45) for the ranking of the 25 most awarded countries in the world in 2005.

And the top two are the same, and in the same order, for the 7th year in a row. USA, 196 points total (137 TV, 59 Print) and Great Britain, 184 points (119 TV, 65 Print).

However, the gap, just 12 points, is the smallest it ever has been. And, more importantly, the US total is the smallest it ever has been. 196 total points compares to 234 in 2004, and 299 in 2003. Part of the reason is that juries at the US-based global/quasi-global shows (of course these juries consist of non-US as well as US jurors, but are usually US-led) have been particularly tough on their own work in 2005. Especially so in Print.

For instance, in Print, out of 33 gold and silver winners at One Show, 4 were USA. At Clios, out of 38 gold and silver, 1(!) was from the USA. In comparison, at D&AD, out of 24 print silvers and nominations, 14 were for Great Britain.

In TV, it's not so extreme, but the tendency is the same. At One Show, out of 33 Best of Show, gold, silver and bronze winners, 11 were USA. At Clios out of 54 Grand Clio, gold and silver winners, 25 were USA (still less than half). But at D&AD, out of 32 golds, silvers and nominations, 23 were for Great Britain.

France and Germany, as in 2004, claimed 3rd and 4th places in the Table. Both had their highest point totals ever with 109 winner points France and 102 winner points Germany. This confirmed the balance of power shift we noted last year in favour of "mainstream Europe" and away from "the Latin bloc", France and Germany only having been in the Top 5 once each prior to 2004 with Brazil, Spain and Argentina from 1999-2003 traditionally slugging it out for places 3rd to 5th.

In 2005, Thailand even kept them out of that. Thailand came 5th with a total of exactly 100 points – following 73 in 2004, with their highest annual score prior to that being 57.

Argentina and Brazil took 6th and 7th places in 2005. It was the third member of "the Latin bloc" that fell away most sharply. Spain, 3rd in the Table with 103 points back in 2001, declined to 12th with 47 points, their lowest ever.

The rest of the Top 10 in 2005 were 8th: Canada – 67 points (their highest ever and comparing to just 12 points in the first year of The Gunn Report back in 1999). 9th: Japan – 57 points, 10th: Australia – 56 points (also a highest ever and maybe the outset of a long trek back to the glories of the 90's when Australia was one of the most awarded advertising markets in the world).

After 7 years of The Gunn Report there are 17 markets in the world that have *always* been in the Top 25 Table. In 7 years consolidated rank order these 17 are: USA, Great Britain, Brazil, Argentina, France, Spain, Germany, Thailand, Japan, Singapore, Canada, Australia, South Africa, The Netherlands, Sweden, Hong Kong and New Zealand.

Following them: the "*nearly always*" group are: Mexico, Czech Republic and Italy (all three of them 6 years out of 7, and every year but 1999); plus Norway (6); Portugal (6); Chile (5) and Poland (5). The "*more than oncers*" group features India (3 years out of 7); Belgium (3, these being the last 3 years); Malaysia (2, these being the last 2 years); China (2) and Switzerland (2). The "*occasionals*" group consists of: Austria, Colombia, Denmark, Slovenia and Uruguay, who've all been in Table Three once.

All in all 2005 has been more than usually volatile, posing questions for the next few years such as the following. Can GB ever catch the US – or will US judges become a tad more patriotic again? Will France and Germany maintain their upward surges? Or will Brazil and Argentina reassert hegemony of the Latin bloc? Can Thailand go any higher? And Canada? Will Australia consolidate their impressive upward trend? And Mexico? And Malaysia? And how soon before India and China progress from "more than oncers" to fully-fledged regulars in the Table? And which will be the next markets in the world, over and above the 34 who've already done so, to make their debuts in Table Three.

Watch this space in The Gunn Report 2006 for at least some of the answers.

How does he know?

A lot of scientific research has been done to find out how a bird on the beach knows there's a worm in the sand. Some thought it had something to do with sound. Others would say it was the smell. There are even stories about tapping on the ground so the worm comes up. So much for the theories.

Fact is, a bird has a simple routine. It just picks and picks. And picks. Nothing else to do all day. No scanning the area. No mappings. No x- and y-axes. Just pick and pick. Up and down. Not really knowing why. Just born to do that. And only surviving because sometimes, by pure coincidence, it hits a big one.

DUVAL GUILLAUME

Brussels - Antwerp - New York

www.duvalguillaume.com

4 • Advertisers

Table Four presents the Top 25 Advertisers in the world in 2005.

The top five advertisers remain the same as in 2004, but the order has changed. The gap between sportswear giants adidas and Nike has widened with adidas scoring their highest tally ever since The Gunn Report started in 1999 and Nike registering their lowest.

In equal 4th place, with 23 points, were Honda and Nike. Honda accrued the vast majority of their points from the UK and the fabulous "Grrr" ad.

Nike had a wide spread of countries contributing to their total – Argentina, Australia, Canada, China, Great Britain, Taiwan and USA – but there was no one big campaign to push their total up towards their previous 30+ highs (highest being 54 in 2002 when they topped the table).

34 points was enough for Sony to take 3rd place (same position as last year although their tally for 2004 was higher at 51). Great Britain provided most of the points for TV and France continued to lead the way with Print. Congratulations also go to UAE for scoring their first ever Gunn Report points with great print work for Sony Wega Engine TV. Other countries contributing to the total were Japan, Singapore and Spain.

With a leap of 13 points to 47 points and 2nd in the Table is adidas. Consolidating on their resurgence last year, they scored their highest ever total (previous high was 33 last year) with Japan leading the way in Print and The Netherlands and USA sharing the spoils in TV.

And so to the accolade of The Most Awarded Advertiser in the World in 2005. With a whopping 65 points (their highest since 1999) Volkswagen remains untouchable at the top of the Table, winning their 6th first place in seven years. Once again they have proved strong in both TV and Print – notably excelling in TV was Germany and in Print, Great Britain scooped most points. 9 different countries contributed to the total – Argentina, Brazil, France, Germany, Great Britain, Mexico, The Netherlands, Singapore and Spain.

6th place, on 20 points was Axe (+ Lynx). In 7th, up from 21st= last year, was an impressive performance from Virgin with 17 points. 8th with 15 points was Coca-Cola and in 9th equal place with 14 points were newcomer Canadian Short Film Festival and Pepsi.

13 of the advertisers in Table Four made it into the Top 25 in 2004. Notable absences were Budweiser and Audi who failed to make the Table for the first time, leaving Nike, Sony and Volkswagen as the only advertisers who have made it into the Top 25 for all seven years of The Gunn Report.

However, our table of consistent performers continues to grow. These advertisers produce award winning work out of a range of different agencies and different markets year after year. So, of particular interest to all the new business directors out there, here's the comprehensive list of those who've made our Table Four in two or more years and in two or more markets (number of years in brackets):

Nike (7)	McDonald's (5)	MTV (3)
Sony (7)	Coca-Cola (4)	Virgin (3)
Volkswagen (7)	Guinness (4)	FedEx (2)
adidas (6)	Heineken (4)	Honda (2)
Audi (6)	Ikea (4)	Land Rover (2)
Budweiser (6)	Levi's (4)	Mattel (2)
Pepsi (6)	Mercedes-Benz (4)	Miller (2)
Axe (+Lynx) (5)	The Economist (4)	Peugeot (2)
BMW (5)	Toyota (4)	Renault (2)
Fox (5)	Mini (3)	

5 • Production Companies

Table Five presents the 25 most awarded production companies in the world in 2005.

By 2004 only 5 production companies had made it into the Top 25 each year of The Gunn Report. The good news is that all 5 are still there in 2005, albeit with a slip down the rankings in most cases. Congratulations for making it into the world's Top 25 all 7 years in a row go to (in alphabetical order):

@radical.media
Gorgeous Enterprises
Hungry Man
Matching Studio
Partizan

One production company should be singled out for further praise as they have not only been in the Top 25 of Table 5 for all 7 years in a row but have stayed in the Top 5 for all 7 years of The Gunn Report: @radical.media.

A wider range of production companies seem to be getting multiple award winning briefs in 2005 with 11 companies achieving 15 or more points this year as opposed to just 6 in 2004 and the cut off point for Table Five was the highest ever at 9 points. 14 production companies in the Top 25 in 2005 were in the table in 2004, with 8 newcomers (3 from Toronto, 2 from London and 1 each from Buenos Aires, Los Angeles and Paris) and 1 re-entry.

5th in 2005, on 22 points, came Large (London). Having dropped out of Table 5 in 2004 they stormed back with some great work, most notably NSPCC "Ventriloquist" , Sony PlayStation 2 "Athletes"/"Golfers" & campaign and The British Heart Foundation "Artery" as well as ads for Double Velvet, RSPCA and Transport for London Teen Road Safety.

Just one point ahead in equal 3rd place came Biscuit Filmworks (Los Angeles) and Nexus (London) on 23 points. Biscuit Filmworks, improving on their 14 points and 7th place last year, produced work for a whole raft of blue chip clients, including adidas, Bud Light, Axe Deodorant, California Milk Advisory Board and eBay

In contrast, Nexus, who join Table 5 for the first time, gained most of their 23 points for one monster ad – Honda Diesel "Grrr". No doubt they will be awarded many more briefs on the strength of their work for Honda so expect to see them again in the Top 25.

2nd in the world in 2005, on 26 points, was @radical.media. This was one place higher than 2004, even though they scored 10 more points last year. As usual there were contributions from their offices all over the world – London, New York, Paris, Sydney and Berlin. Their biggest winner came from Paris for INPES Passive Smoking Awareness but a whole range of top flight clients also contributed to the total, including FedEx, Pepsi, Toyota, Virgin, Visa and Volkswagen.

The clear winner in Table 5, by a margin of 13 points, on 39 points and therefore The Most Awarded Production Company in The World in 2005, was Phenomena (Bangkok). Having first entered the Top 25 in 2002, Phenomena has made steady progress up the Table with top 5 places in both 2003 and 2004. Their much deserved first place included work for no less than 16 different clients – Energy Policy and Planning Office Thailand, Ford Ranger Opencab, Thai Health Promotion Board, Thailand Yellow Pages and Unif Green Tea – to name just a sample.

NO ONE GETS YOUR MESSAGE IN FRONT OF MORE INTERNATIONAL AGENCY PRODUCERS CREATIVES, PRODUCTION EXECUTIVES DIRECTORS AND BIDDERS THAN BOARDS MAGAZINE

THE CREATIVE EDGE IN COMMERCIAL PRODUCTION

A PUBLICATION OF BRUNICO COMMUNICATIONS INC

™Boards is a trademark of Brunico Communications Inc.

TO MARKET YOUR COMPANY, CREATIVE TALENT AND PRODUCTION SERVICES CONTACT US AT +1 (416) 408 2300 or sales@boardsmag.com

6 • Directors

Table Six presents the 25 (27 this year due to 3 x 25th equals) most awarded Directors in the world in 2005.

As highlighted in our previous reports, Table Six is volatile by nature with points going to those Directors favoured with the assignment of working on the most awarded productions. Only 9 directors out of the 27 in 2005 were in the table in 2004, 13 directors registered in the Top 25 in 2005 for the first time and 5 made a re-appearance.

We now have only 2 directors who have made it into the top 25 of Table Six all 7 years of The Gunn Report. So huge congratulations go to Frank Budgen and Suthon Petchsuwan for their remarkable achievement.

In equal 4th place with 19 points were Daniel Kleinman (Great Britain) and Suthon Petchsuwan (Thailand). Daniel Kleinman made a welcome return to Table Six having dropped out of the top 25 in 2004 after coming 1st in 2003. His two big wins were for NSPCC "Ventriloquist" and Sony PlayStation 2 "Athletes"/"Golfers" & campaign. Points were also awarded for British Heart Foundation and Transport for London Teen Road Safety.

Suthon Petchsuwan dropped from his 1st position in 2004 but underlined why he is one of only 2 directors to appear in Table Six for all 7 years of The Gunn Report with ads for 7 different clients, most notably Soken DVD and Unif Green Tea which continued their winning runs started in 2004.

3 points ahead on 22 points and in 2nd equal place were Adam Foulkes and Alan Smith (Great Britain) and Noam Murro (USA). Adam Foulkes and Alan Smith entered Table Six for the first time and were responsible for the most awarded commercial of the year, Honda Diesel "Grrr". They also directed the Observer Music Monthly "From Abba to Zappa" ad.

Noam Murro from Biscuit Filmworks in Los Angeles achieved his highest ever placing in Table Six (previous highest was 10= last year and in 1999). As well as directing adidas "Carry" and California Milk Board "Russian Family" he worked for a whole range of award winning clients including Axe Deodorant, Bud Light, eBay, Holiday Inn and Levi's.

In first place and therefore The Most Awarded Director in The World in 2005, was Thanonchai Sornsrivichai (Thailand). It was the second time he has hit top spot (1st = in 2003 with Daniel Kleinman) and with 37 points it was the second highest winning total since The Gunn Report began in 1999 (highest being Frank Budgen on 44 points in 2002). Working for Phenomena in Bangkok he was responsible for the 3 commercials/campaigns from Thailand in Table One – Thai Health Promotion Board campaign, Ford Ranger Opencab "King Kong", and Thai Energy Policy Office campaign - along with a whole host of ads for 11 other clients. Congratulations to a thoroughly deserving winner.

7 • Agencies

Table 7 (pages 53 & 55) presents the 50 (or 56 to be precise, as we had 9 x 48th equals) most awarded advertising agencies in the world in 2005.

The 48th equals have 9 winner points each. So Agencies on 8 points, who have got into Table 7 of The Gunn Report every year except last year, missed the cut again in 2005. The bar has gotten higher.

All the more reason to state the point that all of the companies who ever make it into Table Seven are terrific advertising agencies – it must be a joy to work in any of them.

Jacques Séguéla – in June 2003 when the Havas board endorsed the sentiment of the paragraph above by announcing Euro 1.5 million annually to be divided among the creatives at those Havas Group agencies who get into The Gunn Report's Table 7 – invented a name for them – "The Top 50 Club".

By 2003 (after the first four years of The Gunn Report, 1999 to 2002), exactly 100 agencies anywhere in the world had ever been in our Table 7 and thus entered the ranks of "The Top 50 Club". In 2003, 15 more joined them, raising the roster to 115. And in 2004 11 more joined them, bringing membership up to 126.

And here's a big welcome to those new members – this year there's only 6 of them – inducted as a result of Table 7 in our 2005 Report – who've brought the roll call of honour up to 132:

BBDO Singapore
Creative Juice/G1 (Bangkok)
DDB Germany
Euro RSCG (London)
M&C Saatchi (Sydney)
Rethink (Vancouver)

The noblest of them all, of course, are those agencies who have made Table 7 every single year. Last year six of them fell away, and after 6 years of The Gunn Report, there were only 9 agencies left anywhere in the world who had been in the Top 50 in the world for all 6 years in a row. In 2005, every single one of these nine survived the global game of musical chairs, and appeared yet again in the Table. These noble nine (in alphabetical order) are:

Top 50 in the World All 7 Years in a Row
AlmapBBDO (Sao Paulo)
AMV.BBDO (London)
Arnold Worldwide (Boston)
Bartle Bogle Hegarty (London)
DDB (Madrid & Barcelona)
DDB (London)
Dentsu (Tokyo & Osaka)
Fallon (Minneapolis & NY)
Lowe (London)

Campbell | Mithun

7 • **Agencies** *cont.*

In 2005, there were exactly 10 agencies in the whole world who scored over 20 winner points. The Year's Top 10 are:

In 10th place with 21 points, TBWA\Chiat\Day, USA. In 9th place, their colleagues who share all their honours on adidas, 180 Amsterdam (180\TBWA).

One point above on 23 points, came DDB (Germany) – highest placed of the Top 50 Club inductees, and Wieden+Kennedy (London) – an inductee in 2004, when they jumped straight into the Table in second place.

6th in the Table, with their highest finish yet, was Del Campo Nazca Saatchi & Saatchi, Buenos Aires. Their 24 points were 7 for TV and 17 for Print and two most awarded Clients were Procter & Gamble and Buenos Aires Zoo.

Coming to the Top 5, no fewer than 4 of them have been previous winners of Table 7. Crispin Porter + Bogusky, Miami, (top of this Table in 2003) took 5th place in 2005 with 26 points: American Legacy Foundation ("Truth" campaign), Molson Canadian, Mini & Mini Cooper, Virgin Atlantic, Burger King and Ikea were among the Clients contributing.

DDB London (top of the Table in our first year 1999) came fourth, for the second year in a row in 2005, with 27 points. Most awarded Clients were Volkswagen (of course), Harvey Nichols, Marmite and The Guardian.

Dentsu, Tokyo and Osaka (winner in Table 7 in 2001) took third place in 2005 on 29 points. Among the blue chip Advertisers with whom they amassed this very good total were Ajinomoto Stadium, Hitachi, Lion products, Kincho Insecticides, KDDI, SME Records and Tower Records, Staff Service Recruitment, Suntory and Toho Cinemas.

We then have to jump up 4 more points to get to our Top 2.

On 33 points TBWA\Paris repeated their elevated 2003 ranking to claim 2nd place in 2005. Sony Playstation was their mega-winner in Print, while more points piled up for Bic, K2R Stain Remover, EMI Anti-Piracy, Spontex, Pedigree Dog Treats among others. Their TV points came from Hansaplast Condoms, Responsible Young Drivers road safety and a wonderful new spot for Aides Awareness - "Vibrators".

The winner of Table 7, the most awarded advertising agency in the world in 2005, finished 1 point higher than TBWA\Paris, and was...AlmapBBDO, Sao Paulo, topping Table 7 for the second year in a row.

AlmapBBDO had a great year in Print (as always) plus a great year in TV too, and produced award winning work for what was quite possibly the widest span of top flight advertisers ever – Pepsi, Volkswagen, Gol Linhas Aereas, Veja Magazine, Sao Paulo Alparagatas, Embratel, Whiskas, O'Boticario, Bayer Aspirina, FedEx, Let's Talk Language School and Fundacao Eye Care all being among them.

It was a thrilling finish between our first two. Warmest congratulations to both. And especially to all the wonderful folks at AlmapBBDO, of course, on becoming *the first ever two-time winner* of Table Seven.

To be in the
Gunn Report,
please contact:

MARCUST.JEAN

If you are here,
congratulations!
We probably already
know you.

8 • Agency Networks

And so we arrive at our "headline" table. Table Eight (on page 57). Where the world's top 20 Agency networks are ranked by their performance in the world's 55 top award contests.

In 2004, for the first time, the previously-named "fledgling" networks were included in the table. (Before last year they'd been in a separate table of that name, not included in The Gunn Report, but sometimes shown in presentations.)

Despite having only 5 or 6 offices each (or about twice that in the case of Arnold) the so-called "fledglings" had shown they could compete in global awards tally terms with the major, traditional networks with 150 offices or so. All 4 of the "fledglings" who made the Top 20 Table in 2004 return in 2005:

2005 World Ranking

Wieden+Kennedy	10th
Bartle Bogle Hegarty	=14th
Fallon	17th
Arnold Worldwide	19th

In fact, BBH and Fallon both improved on their 2004 totals. And, based on the criteria of Gunn Report winner points from more than one market and 15 points plus to debut, Table 8 is proud to welcome in 2005:

2005 World Ranking

Springer & Jacoby	18th

In 2004, we singled out three cases of upward mobility in the middle ranks of the table, and all three of them consolidated on this achievement in 2005.

Publicis held on to 14th place and with 24 winner points scored their second highest ever points total. (Just 2 less then last year, which was well over double the year before). And Publicis Conseil, Paris (with 3 selections on The Showreel of The Year 2005) is undergoing a renaissance as a true creative flagship office.

JWT were able to consolidate on their remarkable growth curve since the early years of The Gunn Report. They held on to 9th place in the table with a total of 52 points (compared to 16th and 15th places in 1999 and 2000 and points totals in the 15-16 range).

Euro RSCG, the youngest of the major world networks, moved up to 8th in the Table from 10th with 55 points (7 up on 2004, their previous best ever) – stellar performances by BETC Euro RSCG in Paris, Euro RSCG Flagship in Bangkok and Euro RSCG London were a key factor in this.

Continuing upwards, Lowe shrugged off some setbacks in the course of the year to hold onto 7th place in the Table.

Ogilvy & Mather slipped a bit to 6th with 70 points from their highest ever finish at 4th place in 2004. This was still a commendable performance, with Asian offices once again providing the lion's share of points, for their 2nd equal highest ranking in the Table.

Leo Burnett (who were top of Table 8 in 2001) moved up a place from 6th to 5th, with 81 points compared to 74 last year. Burnett's big competitive plus is their strength in depth (see below) with good creative offices in all corners of the globe – their biggest hitters in 2005 were Chicago and Prague: but Sao Paulo, Lima, Singapore, Kuala Lumpur, Hong Kong, Paris, London, Madrid. Milan, Buenos Aires and Budapest all supported strongly.

Saatchi & Saatchi with 108 points in 2005, moved up from 5th to 4th and notched up their 7th year out of seven in Table Eight's Top 5. They had stellar performances in all world regions. Buenos Aires led the charge and their Bangkok, Sydney, London and Sao Paulo offices all also featured among the world's Top 50 agencies, with Auckland, Mexico City and Kuala Lumpur being further strong contributors.

INTERNATIONAL
ADVERTISING
ASSOCIATION

CHALLENGES OF CHANGE ∙ MARCH 20-23 2006

40th IAA WORLD CONGRESS

Rub Shoulders with World Leaders in Communication

Dr. Tony Alessandra	Author of 'The Platinum Rule'
Jose Maria Aznar	Prime Minister of Spain (1996-2004)
Howard Draft	Chairman & CEO, Draft Worldwide
John Elkins	Executive V.P., Visa International
Steve Forbes	CEO of Forbes
Colin Gotlieb	Chief Executive, OMD Europe
Donald Gunn	Publisher of 'The Annual Gunn Report & Showreel'
Hameed Haroon	CEO, Dawn Group of Publications, Pakistan
Sahar Hashemi	Co-Founder of Coffee Republic, UK
Bob Isherwood	Worldwide Creative Director, Saatchi & Saatchi
Ken Kaess	President & CEO, DDB Worldwide Communications Group
Jack Klues	Chairman & CEO, Starcom Worldwide
Tateo Mataki	Chief Executive Officer, DENTSU, Japan
Michael Mendenhall	EVP Global Marketing, Walt Disney Parks and Resorts
Marcio Moreira	Vice Chairman/COO, McCann-Erickson World Group
Susannah Outfin	CEO, Carat International
Norman Pearlstine	Editor-in-Chief, Time Inc.
Jerry Rao	CEO, MphaSis, India/USA
Ghassan Salame	Ex-Lebanese Minister of Culture
Mike Simon	Senior Vice President, Corporate Communications, Emirates Airlines
Neil Simpson	Global Brand Director, Vodafone Group
James R. Stengel	Global Marketing Officer, The Procter & Gamble Company
David Taylor	European Business Speaker of the Year 2004
Sergio Zyman	Marketing Visionary, Author and Former CMO, Coca-Cola, USA.

In alphabetical order

For updates and registration, visit www.iaaDubai2006.com

International Advertising Associaton, UAE Chapter, PO Box 71104, 8, Dubai Media City, Dubai, UAE
Tel : +971 4 3903232, Fax: +971 4 3908362, email: iaauae@emirates.net.ae,

IAA/13

8 • Agency Networks *cont.*

The top three in The Gunn Report's Table 8 in 2005 were exactly the same top three as in 2004. But the order changed.

DDB Worldwide came in 3rd in 2005 with 134 points. They were the world's top network in Europe, with London and Berlin both in the world's top 8 agencies plus a strong surge up the table by Paris, a strong performance as usual from Spain and good support from Amsterdam. Canada (both Vancouver and Toronto) had a great year, and Sao Paulo and USA turned in good results as usual with Mexico City and Kuala Lumpur also doing well.

BBDO Worldwide amassed 19 more points than DDB for a total of 153 (79 TV, 74 Print) to finish a strong second in the 2005 table. In addition to AlmapBBDO, Sao Paulo, the most awarded agency in the world in 2005, they had 5 more markets in the world's Top 50 – London, Bangkok, USA (New York plus Chicago), Singapore and Johannesburg. Argentina, Australia, Canada, France, Germany, New Zealand (both Auckland and Wellington) and Spain (both Contrapunto and Tiempo BBDO) also contributed strongly.

A table we introduced last year explains one of the key reasons for BBDO's success:

Number of Markets Contributing to Top 10 Network's Total Score 2005

BBDO	22	Lowe	13
DDB	17	O&M	16
Euro RSCG	8	Saatchi & Saatchi	19
JWT	13	TBWA	15
Leo Burnett	26	Wieden+Kennedy	2

So while Burnett continue to have the most offices capable of world class work (long live the Global Product Committee, as we also said last year), BBDO have the second most and significantly more than their top two competitors for table-winning points – DDB & TBWA.

But back to the business in hand. DDB Worldwide – last year's winner and also our very first winner of Table 8 in 1999 – was the third most awarded Agency Network in the world in 2005 with 134 points. BBDO Worldwide – three times winner of this table in 2000, 2002 and 2003 – was second in 2005 on 153 points.

The winner of Table 8 in The Gunn Report this year, the most awarded agency network in the world in 2005 is...TBWA Worldwide. With the truly excellent total of 160 points. They had no fewer than 5 agencies (3 more than BBDO or DDB) in the world's top 20: TBWA\Paris (2nd), 180 Amsterdam (180\TBWA) (9th), TBWA\Chiat\Day USA (10th) and Creative Juice/G1, Bangkok and TBWA\London (19th equal). Singapore, Tokyo and Johannesburg were also stellar performers. And Madrid, Melbourne, Berlin, Dublin, Helsinki, Vancouver and Vilnius also chipped in priceless points toward their triumphant total.

Who would have thought back in 1970 when four guys – one Greek-American, one French, one Swiss and one Italian – Bill, Claude, Uli and Paolo by name – did a breakaway from Young & Rubicam in Paris to start their own little shop that the result would be a mighty global network?

2005 has been a bit of a milestone year for TBWA Worldwide. They made adidas the new Nike. Jean-Marie stayed. And now there's one further reason for 8500 hearts to rejoice.

TABLE 1

TV & CINEMA

THE MOST AWARDED COMMERCIALS IN THE WORLD IN 2005

			Ad pts
1	HONDA DIESEL • Grrr	Wieden+Kennedy (London)	35
2	ADIDAS • Laila*	180 Amsterdam (180\TBWA)	19
3	CANADIAN SHORT FILM FESTIVAL • Good Cop. Bad Cop / Special FX / Love Story & campaign *	Taxi (Toronto)	15
4=	LYNX 24-7 • Getting Dressed*	Bartle Bogle Hegarty (London)	14
	PEUGEOT 407 • Toys*	BETC Euro RSCG (Paris)	14
6	VOLKSWAGEN GOLF DSG • Kids on Steps	DDB Germany (Berlin)	13
7	NSPCC • Ventriloquist	Saatchi & Saatchi (London)	13
8	ORANGE • Verne Troyer / Patrick Swayze / Sean Astin	Mother (London)	13
9	STELLA ARTOIS • Pilot*	Lowe (London)	13
10	CITROEN C4 • Carbot	Euro RSCG (London)	12
11	VH1 MTV • Parents' Day / Ripe & campaign	La Comunidad (Miami Beach)	12
12	SONY PLAYSTATION 2 • Athletes / Golfers & campaign	TBWA\London	12
13	VIM THICK BLEACH • Prison Visitor*	Zig (Toronto)	12
14	THAI HEALTH PROMOTION / ANTI DRUNKENESS • Bar Fight / Harassment & campaign	Saatchi & Saatchi (Bangkok)	12
15	MERCEDES-BENZ CABRIOLET • Sounds of Summer	Springer & Jacoby (Hamburg)	11
16	FORD RANGER OPEN CAB • King Kong	JWT (Bangkok)	11
17	INPES PASSIVE SMOKING AWARENESS • Marie	FCB (Paris)	10
18	AEROLINEAS ARGENTINAS • Shadow*	JWT (Buenos Aires)	10
19	ADIDAS • Unstoppable	TBWA\Chiat\Day (San Francisco)	10
20	SONY PLAYSTATION 2 • Mountain*	TBWA\London	10

* on The Showreel of The Year 2004

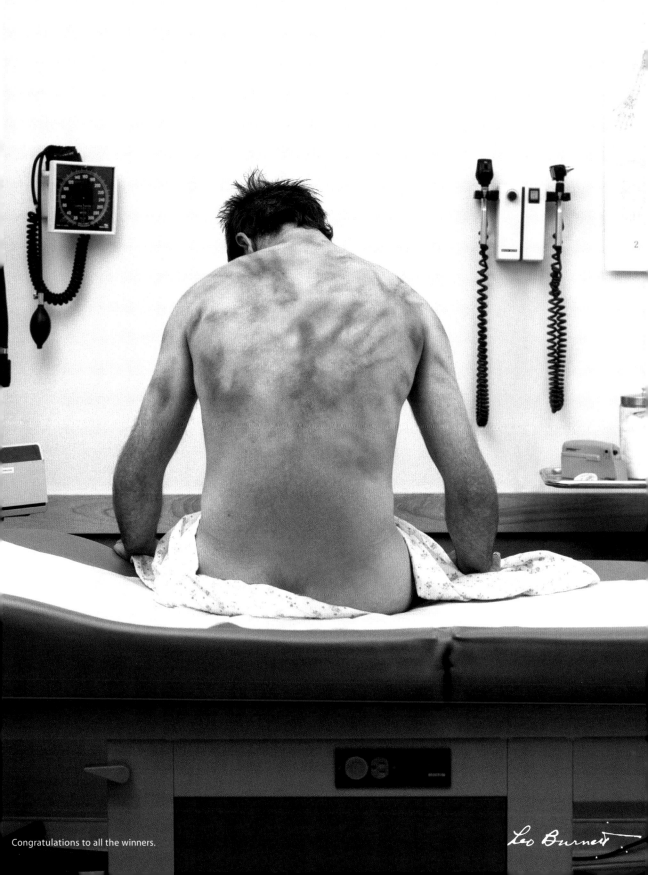

Congratulations to all the winners.

- two guys in an office, dancing.
boss walks in, panicked.
he needs a ton of information from them
(he can't believe they've not already busy
working on it.)
guys stop dancing, instantly get him all
the information with their nextel phones,
then go back to dancing.

nextel. done.

Think it. Disrupt it. Connect it.

TBWA\

TABLE 1

TV & CINEMA cont.

THE MOST AWARDED COMMERCIALS IN THE WORLD IN 2005

Ad pts

21	AJINOMOTO STADIUM • Husky Girls	Dentsu (Tokyo)	9
22	SOKEN DVD PLAYER • Kill Bill Kill Bill / Tititanic / X...X...X*	Euro RSCG Flagship (Bangkok)	9
23	PONLE CORAZON ANNUAL COLLECTION • Magic	Leo Burnett (Lima)	9
24	ENERGIZER BATTERIES • Mano Japanesa	Grupo Gallegos (Long Beach, CA)	9
25	SCIENCE WORLD • Boardroom	Rethink (Vancouver)	9
26	EVIAN • Waterboy	BETC Euro RSCG (Paris)	8
27	ADIDAS • Nadia / Jesse / Haile	180 Amsterdam (180\TBWA)	8
28	RENAULT CLIO • Scarecrow	Lowe A&B (Buenos Aires)	8
29	BONJOUR PARIS LANGUAGE SCHOOL • Heart Attacks	DDB Sao Paulo	8
30	CHARAL MEAT • The Race	Leo Burnett (Paris)	8
31	VOLKSWAGEN GOLF GTI • For Boys Who Were Always Men	DDB Germany (Berlin)	7
32	L'EQUIPE NEWSPAPER • Mother / Child	DDB Paris	7
33	AMERIQUEST MORTAGES • Mini-Mart / Parking Meter & campaign	DDB Los Angeles	7
34	THAI ENERGY POLICY OFFICE • Lost Money / Mousetrap / Madam	Saatchi & Saatchi (Bangkok)	7
35	UNEFON MOBILE PHONE & PHOTOS • Leg	S2 (Mexico City)	7
36	BC LIONS • Vending Machine / Cashier	Rethink (Vancouver)	6
37	H&M STORES • Karl Lagerfeld	Red Room (Stockholm)	6
38	PAMPERS • Stairs / Crying	Del Campo Nazca S&S (B. Aires)	6
39	BUD LIGHT • Real Men of Genius campaign*	DDB Chicago	6
40	AMERICAN LEGACY FOUNDATION • Drill / Voice / Flag*	Arnold (Boston), Crispin PB (Miami)	6
41	ADIDAS • Carry	TBWA\Chiat\Day (San Francisco)	6
42	VIRGIN ATLANTIC • Love Story	Net#work BBDO (Johannesburg)	6
43	SAGEM MYX5-2 MOBILE PHONE • Tokyo	Publicis (Paris)	6
44	CALIFORNIA MILK BOARD • Russian Family	Goodby Silverstein (San Francisco)	6
45	TELECOM ITALIA • Gandhi	Young & Rubicam (Milan)	6
46	TBS NETWORK • Names / Strange Fruit / Wings & campaign*	Publicis (New York)	6
47	NIKE • Evolution	Wieden+Kennedy (Portland, OR)	6
48	BRITISH HEART FOUNDATION/ANTI-SMOKING • Artery*	Euro RSCG (London)	6
49	COCA-COLA • Rivalries	Santo (Buenos Aires)	6
50	COMPANHIA ATHLETICA GYM • Crying*	DDB Sao Paulo	6

* on The Showreel of The Year 2004

This time we come in peace.

TABLE 2

PRINT

THE MOST AWARDED PRINT ADS AND CAMPAIGNS IN THE WORLD IN 2005

			Ad pts
1	TAMIYA MODEL KITS SHOP • Light Bulb / Frog / Watermelon	Creative Juice/G1 (Bangkok)	20
2	ANGLICAN WELFARE COUNCIL • Churchill / Chaplin / Newton	Ogilvy & Mather (Singapore)	19
3	VOLKSWAGEN POLO • King Kong	DDB London	17
4	BISLEY OFFICE EQUIPMENT • Clock / Chaos / Flag	Kolle Rebbe Werbeagentur (Hamburg)	16
5	GRANDE REPORTAGEM MAGAZINE • Flags campaign	FCB Portugal (Lisbon)	15
6	THE ECONOMIST • Light Bulb	AMV.BBDO (London)	13
7	ADIDAS • Impossible Sprint	TBWA\Japan (Tokyo)	13
8	PIZZA HUT DELIVERY • Psycho / Singing in the Rain / The Graduate	BBDO Singapore	12
9	TIME MAGAZINE • Pendulum	Fallon (New York)	12
10	WERU NOISE PROTECTION WINDOWS • Garbage Collection / Rockers / Dogs	Scholz & Friends (Berlin)	12
11	NUGGET SHOE POLISH • Exam Cheat Note / Police Officer	The Jupiter Drawing Room (Jo'burg)	11
12	SMITH & WESSON GUNS • Fly / Moth / Beetle	Springer & Jacoby (Hamburg)	11
13	11 NEWS 1 CHANNEL • Boy / Businessman / Housewife	Euro RSCG Flagship (Bangkok)	11
14	CZECH NATIONAL LIBRARY • The Old Man & The Sea / Jane Eyre & campaign	Leo Burnett (Prague)	10
15	VOLKSWAGEN GOLF GTI • For Boys Who Were Always Men	DDB Germany (Berlin)	10
16	THE AKATU INST. FOR CONSCIOUS CONSUMPTION • Favela	Leo Burnett (Sao Paulo)	9
17	SONY PLAYSTATION 2 • Adultery	TBWA\Paris	9
18	VEJA MAGAZINE • Bin Laden / Bush / Saddam & campaign	AlmapBBDO (Sao Paulo)	9
19	BIC PERMANENT MARKER • Old Lady	TBWA\Paris	9
20	AQUENT BUSINESS SERVICES • Coffee / Corridor / Fuse Box / Video	Leo Burnett (Singapore)	9

THE HOTTEST CREATIVITY
FROM THE MOST CREATIVE REGION IN THE WORLD

1492 CULTURA CREATIVA.

A bimonthly magazine with the most amazing ideas from Ibero-America.

124 pages and a CD of pure creativity.

Award winning cases • Trends • Special reports

1492@fiap.com.ar

1492CC is a publication of the FIAP (Ibero-American Advertising Festival)

TABLE 2

PRINT *cont.*

Ad pts

21	MOLSON CANADIAN • Tools campaign	Crispin Porter + Bogusky (Miami)	8
22	HERRINGBONE TAILORS • Insane Tailors campaign	M&C Saatchi (Sydney)	7
23	DHL COURIERS • Truck	Jung Von Matt (Berlin)	7
24	DDB CANADA (HOUSE) • Bedroom / Kitchen / Living Room	DDB Vancouver	7
25	TESCO SUPERMARKETS • Eggs / Carrots / Soap & campaign	Lowe (London)	7
26	SONY PLAYSTATION 2 • Plugs	TBWA\Paris	7
27	BUENOS AIRES ZOO • Lion / Orangutan / Polar Bear	Del Campo Nazca S&S (Buenos Aires)	7
28	SONY WEGA ENGINE TV • Paper Clip	Tonic Communications (Dubai)	6
29	VOLKSWAGEN COMMERCIAL VEHICLES • Les Dangers campaign	DDB Paris	6
30	ARIEL • Antes Despues campaign	Del Campo Nazca S&S (Buenos Aires)	6
31	K2R STAIN REMOVER • Tie / Shirt / Dress & campaign	TBWA\Paris	6
32	VOLKSWAGEN TOUAREG • Wading Depth	Grabarz & Partners (Hamburg)	6
33	IL VIZIO • Africa / Flood / Navy / Rocket & campaign	M&C Saatchi (Sydney)	6
34	SCOTT PAPER TOWELS • Pork / Chicken / French Fries	JWT (Bangkok)	6
35	NATIONAL PARK WILDLIFE & PLANT CONSERVATION • Axe	Ogilvy & Mather (Bangkok)	5
36	DHL PARCEL DELIVERY SERVICE • 8457 / Interphone / Plants	Ogilvy & Mather (Mexico City)	5
37	BERLITZ INTERNATIONAL • Chinatown	Scholz & Friends (Berlin)	5
38	LIECHTENSTEIN MUSEUM RE-OPENING • Fresco Airport / Fresco Taxi	Wien Nord Pilz (Vienna)	5
39	VIAGRA • Bus Stop / Coffee / Vacuum Cleaner & campaign	DDB Brussels	5
40	BMW X3 • Mix Your Playgrounds campaign	BDDP et Fils (Paris)	5
41	NIKON WIDE LENS CAMERA • School Photo	Naga DDB Malaysia (Kuala Lumpur)	5
42	GOL LINHAS AEREAS • Ahora Todo El Mundo campaign	AlmapBBDO (Sao Paulo)	5
43	LEVI'S 501'S EUROPE • Car / Chair / Door	Bartle Bogle Hegarty (London)	5
44	DOVE SKINCARE PRODUCTS • Questions campaign	Ogilvy & Mather (London)	5
45	SONY PLAYSTATION 2 • Welcome	TBWA\Madrid	5
46	AMNESTY INTERNATIONAL • Soldier Child / Prisoner / Execution	Contrapunto (Madrid)	5
47	VOLKSWAGEN POLO • Cops	DDB London	5
48	NESTLE QUALITY STREET • Windy / Train / Parky	Lowe (London)	5
49	PANADOL • Bushes	Y&R Wunderman (Beijing)	5
50	LAND ROVER • Birds	Ogilvy & Mather (Mexico City)	5

BRAD FORSYTHE   RAY SCHILENS

What this business needs is more BS worth listening to.
THE
ADVERTISING
SHOW

Join thousands of listeners every week by logging onto www.theadvertisingshow.com

They're the hottest radio show on the Internet. Now Brad & Ray are asking you to bust chops and call, write or email the hottest talk radio station in your area and demand they air the hyperpowered Advertising Show for the enjoyment and enlightenment of the ad agency crowd, their clients and the millions of media fans in America. Every weekend, Brad & Ray let it all hang out and burn the airwaves with the business (and monkey business) of people passionate about the ad game. You never thought advertising (or radio) could be this much fun! To listen to the marketing wisdom and biting cultural wit of Brad & Ray, log onto www.theadvertisingshow.com or call the GM of the radio station in your city and tell them if they aren't airing The Advertising Show, we'll send the Energizer Bunny to their station to commit assault and battery!

THE ADVERTISING SHOW
AIRS LIVE SUNDAYS
FROM 5:00PM TO 7:00PM ET
LISTEN LIVE ONLINE:
WWW.THEADVERTISINGSHOW.COM
SPONSORED BY

PODCASTS
RSS FEEDS
NOW AVAILABLE

TABLE 3

COUNTRIES

THE MOST AWARDED COUNTRIES IN THE WORLD IN 2005

		Winner Pts TV	Winner Pts Print	TOTAL
1	USA (1)	137	59	196
2	Great Britain (2)	119	65	184
3	France (3)	60	49	109
4	Germany (4)	46	56	102
5	Thailand (7)	68	32	100
6	Argentina (5=)	63	31	94
7	Brazil (5=)	44	36	80
8	Canada (10)	48	19	67
9	Japan (11)	45	12	57
10	Australia (12)	31	25	56
11	Singapore (8)	6	47	53
12	Spain (9)	28	19	47
13	The Netherlands (13)	34	3	37
14	Mexico (15=)	26	9	35
15	South Africa (14)	11	22	33
16	Malaysia (17)	6	16	22
17	New Zealand (15=)	4	13	17
18	Italy (18)	14	1	15
19	Czech Republic (19)	6	8	14
20=	Belgium (20=)	7	6	13
	Chile (-)	3	10	13
22	Sweden (20=)	9	3	12
23=	China (-)	6	5	11
	Norway (-)	10	1	11
25=	Hong Kong (20=)	3	6	9
	Portugal (-)	1	8	9

(numbers in brackets ( )= ranking 2004)

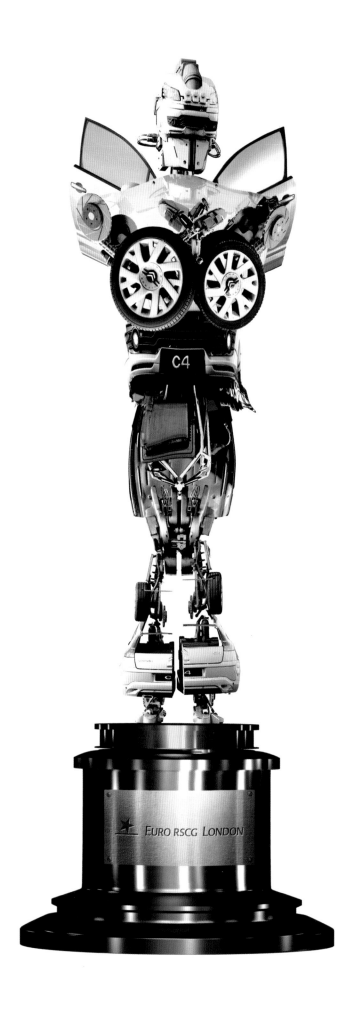

TABLE 4

ADVERTISERS

THE MOST AWARDED ADVERTISERS IN THE WORLD IN 2005

		Winner Pts TV	Winner Pts Print	TOTAL
1	Volkswagen (1)	26	39	65
2	adidas (4)	39	8	47
3	Sony (3)	19	15	34
4=	Honda (3)	23	-	23
	Nike (5)	17	6	23
6	Axe (+ Lynx) (7=)	18	2	20
7	Virgin (21=)	11	6	17
8	Coca-Cola (17=)	14	1	15
9=	Canadian Short Film Festival (-)	14	-	14
	Pepsi (-)	9	5	14
11=	Buenos Aires Zoo (-)	1	12	13
	Tamiya Model Kits Shop (-)	-	13	13
13=	American Legacy Foundation (12=)	6	5	11
	Anglican Welfare Council (-)	-	11	11
	BMW (10)	4	7	11
	Levi's (-)	8	3	11
	Mini (9)	2	9	11
	Peugeot (-)	11	-	11
	Renault (-)	11	-	11
	Thai Health Promotion Board (-)	11	-	11
	Unif Green Tea (24=-)	11	-	11
22=	Mercedes-Benz (-)	10	-	10
	Pizza Hut (-)	-	10	10
24=	The Economist (24=)	-	9	9
	Unefon (-)	9	-	9

(numbers in brackets ( )= ranking 2004)

SHOOT®

The Leading News and
Information Source for
Commercial, Interactive &
Branded Content
Production.

Your connection
to the world
of great work
and the people
behind it.

www.shootonline.com

TABLE 5

PRODUCTION COMPANIES

THE MOST AWARDED PRODUCTION COMPANIES IN THE WORLD IN 2005

		Winner pts
1	Phenomena (Bangkok) (5)	39
2	@radical.media (London, Paris, Berlin, Sydney, New York) (3)	26
3=	Biscuit Filmworks (Los Angeles) (7)	23
	Nexus (London) (-)	23
5	Large (London) (-)	22
6	Matching Studio (Bangkok) (4)	20
7=	MJZ (Los Angeles, New York, London) (12=)	19
	Hungry Man (Los Angeles, New York) (6)	19
9	Park Pictures (New York) (15)	18
10	Reginald Pike (Toronto) (-)	16
11	Stink (London) (8=)	15
12	Garcia Bross (Mexico City) (11)	14
13=	Gorgeous Enterprises (London) (2)	13
	Partizan (London, Los Angeles) (1)	13
	Pioneer Productions (Buenos Aires) (-)	13
	Untitled (Toronto) (-)	13
17	Cobblestone Filmproduktion (Hamburg) (-)	12
18	Landia Republica (Buenos Aires) (17=)	11
19=	Small Family Business (London) (-)	10
	Smuggler (Los Angeles) (-)	10
	Spy Films (Toronto) (-)	10
	Tohokushinsha (Tokyo) (21=)	10
	Wanda Productions (La Plaine Saint-Denis) (-)	10
24=	Czar (Amsterdam, Brussels, New York) (8=)	9
	Jodaf Mixer (Sao Paulo) (21=)	9

(numbers in brackets ( )= ranking 2004)

You're on location.
Your camera jams. Your
crew are being deported for
not having work permits.
You've just found out
tomorrow's a bank holiday.
No one told you about the
actors strike. Worse still...
you're behind schedule and
you're stuck in the hotel from
hell.

If you'd like your shoot to run a little more smoothly, just flip
open The Location Guide, or log on at www.thelocationguide.com.
It's your one stop pre-production and planning tool for any
kind of shoot...big, small, or potentially disastrous.

TABLE 6

DIRECTORS

THE MOST AWARDED DIRECTORS IN THE WORLD IN 2005

		Winner pts
1	Thanonchai Sornsrivichai (Thailand) (2)	37
2=	Adam Foulkes / Alan Smith (Great Britain) (-)	22
	Noam Murro (USA) (10=)	22
4=	Daniel Kleinman (Great Britain) (-)	19
	Suthon Petchsuwan (Thailand) (1)	19
6	Lance Acord (USA) (10=)	18
7	Tim Godsall (Canada) (-)	15
8=	Simon Bross (Mexico) (20=)	14
	Luciano Podkaminsky (Argentina) (-)	14
10	Ivan Zacharias (Great Britain) (7=)	11
11=	Bryan Buckley (USA) (-)	10
	Andy Fogwill (Argentina) (20=)	10
13=	Agustin Alberdi (Argentina) (-)	9
	Neill Blomkamp (Canada) (-)	9
	Ringan Ledwidge (Great Britain) (-)	9
	Sebastian Strasser (Germany) (-)	9
17=	Philippe Andre (France) (-)	8
	Remy Belvaux (France) (-)	8
	Les Elvis (France) (20=)	8
	Frank Budgen (Great Britain) (3=)	8
	Craig Gillespie (USA) (-)	8
	Ulf Johansson (USA & Great Britain) (-)	8
	The Perlorian Brothers (Canada) (-)	8
	Ole Peters / Timo Schaedel (Germany) (-)	8
25=	Javier Blanco (Argentina) (-)	7
	Armando Bo (Argentina) (-)	7
	Johan Renck (France & Sweden) (-)	7

(numbers in brackets ( )= ranking 2004)

-REPEAT AFTER ME. I'M A WINNER
-I'M A WINNER !
-I'M A WINNER
-I'M A WINNER !
-I'M A WHAT ?
-A WINNER !
-A WHAT ?
-A WINNER !
-AND WHERE WILL I BE NEXT YEAR ?
-ON THE RIGHT HAND PAGE !
-WELL DONE

-I'M A WINNER !

✴ BETC EURO RSCG
+33 (0)156 41 39 95

TABLE 7

AGENCIES

THE MOST AWARDED AGENCIES IN THE WORLD IN 2005

		Winner Pts TV	Winner Pts Print	TOTAL
1	AlmapBBDO (Sao Paulo) (1)	14	20	34
2	TBWA\Paris (5)	4	29	33
3	Dentsu (Tokyo & Osaka) (6)	28	1	29
4	DDB London (4)	4	23	27
5	Crispin Porter + Bogusky (Miami) (3)	10	16	26
6	Del Campo Nazca Saatchi & Saatchi (Buenos Aires) (41=)	7	17	24
7=	DDB Germany (Berlin) (-)	12	11	23
	Wieden+Kennedy (London) (2)	23	-	23
9	180 Amsterdam (180\TBWA) (14)	22	-	22
10	TBWA\Chiat\Day (S. Francisco, New York, LA) (7)	21	-	21
11	Lowe (London) (19=)	11	9	20
12	Bartle Bogle Hegarty (London) (32=)	16	3	19
13=	Euro RSCG Flagship (Bangkok) (12)	10	8	18
	Taxi (Toronto) (-)	14	4	18
15=	BETC Euro RSCG (Paris) (22=)	16	1	17
	Fallon (Minneapolis & New York) (37=)	7	10	17
	Saatchi & Saatchi (Bangkok) (22=)	17	-	17
	Springer & Jacoby (Hamburg) (-)	11	6	17
19=	Abbott Mead Vickers.BBDO (London) (37=)	5	11	16
	Creative Juice/G1 (Bangkok) (-)	4	12	16
	TBWA\London (11)	16	-	16
22	BBDO Bangkok (8)	14	1	15
23=	DDB Canada (Toronto & Vancouver) (32=)	3	11	14
	DDB Paris (41=)	5	9	14
25=	Goodby Silverstein & Partners (San Francisco) (-)	11	2	13
	Saatchi & Saatchi (Sydney) (41=)	8	5	13

(numbers in brackets ( )= ranking 2004)

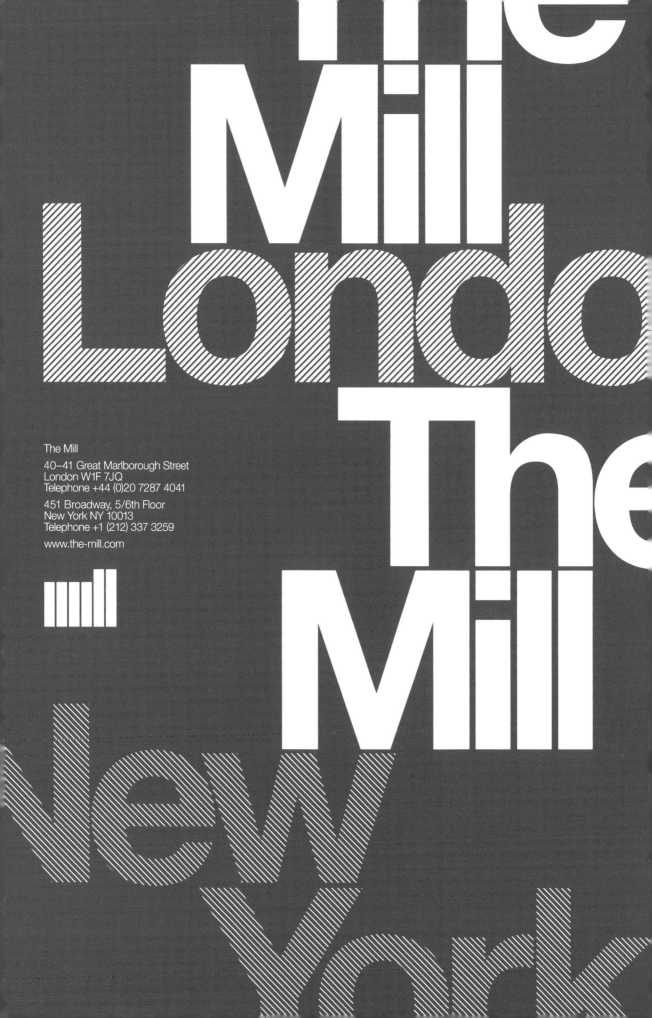

The
Mill
London
The
Mill
New York

The Mill

40–41 Great Marlborough Street
London W1F 7JQ
Telephone +44 (0)20 7287 4041

451 Broadway, 5/6th Floor
New York NY 10013
Telephone +1 (212) 337 3259

www.the-mill.com

TABLE 7

AGENCIES *cont.*

THE MOST AWARDED AGENCIES IN THE WORLD IN 2005

	Winner Pts TV	Winner Pts Print	TOTAL
27= La Comunidad (Miami Beach) (15=)	11	1	12
Mother (London) (-)	11	1	12
Ogilvy & Mather (Singapore) (17=)	-	12	12
Rethink (Vancouver) (-)	10	2	12
TBWA\Singapore (27=)	-	12	12
32= BBDO (New York & Chicago) (41=)	9	2	11
BBDO Singapore (-)	-	11	11
DDB Brasil (41=)	11	-	11
Net#work BBDO (Johannesburg) (22=)	4	7	11
Ogilvy & Mather (Bangkok) (-)	7	4	11
S2 (Mexico City) (32=)	10	1	11
Wieden+Kennedy (Portland, OR) (19=)	11	-	11
Young & Rubicam (Buenos Aires) (-)	7	4	11
40= Arnold Worldwide (Boston) (9=)	5	5	10
Euro RSCG (London) (-)	10	-	10
Jung Von Matt (Hamburg & Berlin) (15=)	6	4	10
Leo Burnett (Chicago) (17=)	4	6	10
Ogilvy & Mather (Buenos Aires) (41=)	9	1	10
Saatchi & Saatchi (London) (-)	8	2	10
Scholz & Friends (Berlin) (37=)	-	10	10
TBWA\Japan (41=)	-	10	10
48= DDB (Chicago, LA & San Francisco) (9=)	9	-	9
DDB Espana (27=)	3	6	9
F/Nazca Saatchi & Saatchi (Sao Paulo) (-)	7	2	9
Hakuhodo (Tokyo & Osaka) (-)	8	1	9
JWT (Buenos Aires) (27=)	8	1	9
Kolle Rebbe Werbeagentur (Hamburg) (13)	1	8	9
Leo Burnett (Prague) (-)	3	6	9
Lowe A&B (Buenos Aires) (-)	8	1	9
M&C Saatchi (Sydney) (-)	-	9	9

The F&B Network

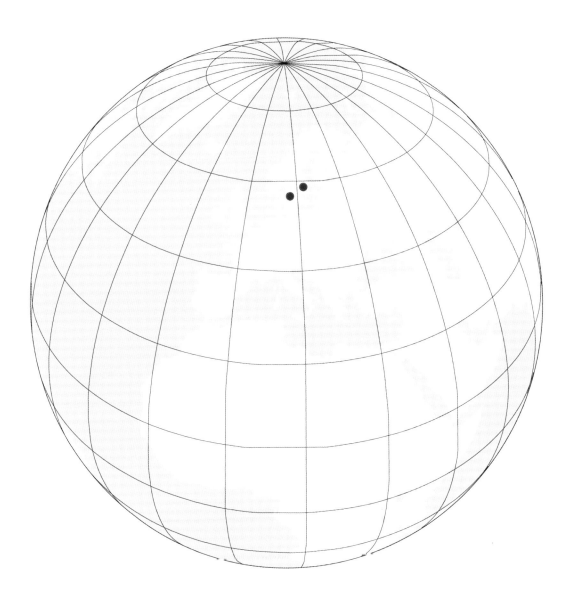

Forsman & Bodenfors / Göteborg +46 31 17 67 30 / Stockholm, +46 8 411 77 11 / **www.fb.se**

TABLE 8

AGENCY NETWORKS

THE TOP 20 AGENCY NETWORKS IN THE WORLD IN 2005

		Winner Pts TV	Winner Pts Print	TOTAL
1	TBWA WORLDWIDE (2)	83	77	160
2	BBDO WORLDWIDE (3)	79	74	153
3	DDB WORLDWIDE (1)	61	73	134
4	SAATCHI & SAATCHI (5)	66	42	108
5	LEO BURNETT (6)	37	44	81
6	OGILVY & MATHER (4)	26	44	70
7	LOWE (7=)	39	20	59
8	EURO RSCG (10)	44	11	55
9	JWT (9)	35	17	52
10	WIEDEN+KENNEDY (7=)	34	-	34
11	DENTSU (12)	28	2	30
12	YOUNG & RUBICAM (15)	16	12	28
13	FCB (18)	17	10	27
14=	BARTLE BOGLE HEGARTY (16)	19	5	24
	PUBLICIS (14)	17	7	24
16	McCANN-ERICKSON (11)	17	6	23
17	FALLON (17)	12	10	22
18	SPRINGER & JACOBY (-)	12	6	18
19	ARNOLD WORLDWIDE (13)	9	5	14
20	GREY (19)	6	3	9
(All Others)		(222)	(124)	(346)
TOTAL		879	592	1471

(numbers in brackets after each name = ranking 2004)

"Action, suspense and intrigue. Jubilation and despair. Another Thursday morning with *Campaign*. I love it."

Kelly Clark, Chief Executive, Mindshare UK

Advertising: christina.wadsworth@haynet.com
+44 (0) 20 8267 4920

Subscriptions: victoria.mcdougall@haynet.com
+44 (0) 20 8267 4914

campaign

The Gunn Report 2005 Summary

i **Commercial or TV/Cinema Campaign of the Year:**

Honda Diesel • Grrr   Wieden+Kennedy (London)

Runners up: adidas • Laila - 180 Amsterdam (180/TBWA) &
Canadian Short Film Festival • Good Cop. Bad Cop / Special FX / Love Story & campaign - Taxi (Toronto)

ii **Print Ad or Campaign of the Year:**

Tamiya Model Kits Shop • Light Bulb / Frog / Watermelon   Creative Juice/G1 (Bangkok)

Runners up: Anglican Welfare Council • Churchill / Chaplin / Newton - O&M Singapore &
Volkswagen Polo • King Kong - DDB London

iii **Country of the Year:**

USA

Runners up: Great Britain & France

iv **Advertiser of the Year:**

Volkswagen

Runners up: adidas & Sony

v **Production Company of the Year:**

Phenomena (Bangkok)

Runners up: @radical.media (London, Paris, Berlin, Sydney, New York) &
Biscuit Filmworks (Los Angeles); Nexus (London)

vi **Director of the Year:**

Thanonchai Sornsrivichai (Thailand)

Runners up: Adam Foulkes/Alan Smith (Great Britain); Noam Murro (USA)

vii **Agency of the Year:**

AlmapBBDO (Sao Paulo)

Runners up: TBWA\Paris & Dentsu (Tokyo & Osaka)

viii **Agency Network of the Year:**

TBWA Worldwide

Runners up: BBDO Worldwide & DDB Worldwide

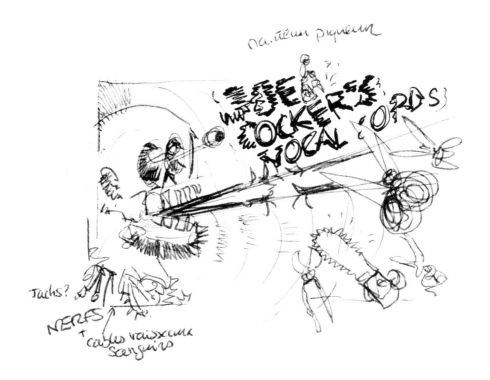

Think it. Disrupt it. Connect it.

TBWA\

A Note on Methodology

The idea behind The Gunn Report is to combine the winners' lists from all the most important award shows, everywhere in the world. Some of these are global contests, some regional, some national. For the year 2005 Report, we are including the top 34 shows in the world for TV & Cinema, and the top 21 for Print.

We have continued to be secretive about what these shows are. For a few good reasons, the most important being not to upset any friends - award contest entrepreneurs around the world - whose shows might be among those not included.

Regarding the national shows, what we can say is that these are included for the 17 most important creative advertising markets - the ones where any aspiring creative network has to aim to be a player. We include the main national show(s) in the USA, Great Britain, France, Germany, Japan, Brazil, Spain, Australia (which includes New Zealand), Greater China, Argentina, Canada, Italy, Mexico, The Netherlands, South Africa, Sweden and Thailand.

The inclusion of more shows for TV and Cinema than for Print is deliberate. TV is still the front line in our business. Also many shows that honour both tend to give more awards to Print than TV.* The 2005 points reflect a 60% : 40% TV : Print split.

The level of award that counts for a given show is "Cannes Bronze Lion Equivalent". The application of this is a bit judgmental but the decisions are usually pretty obvious, and the level of prize can vary from year to year for the same show, if a jury has been mega-generous or mega-stingy.

Winner points, which apply for Tables Three to Eight (Countries, Brands, Production Companies, Directors, Agencies and Agency Networks), are different from Ad Points, which apply for Tables One and Two (Commercials and Print Ads).

"Winner Points" are awarded as 1 point for each win at the qualifying level at a qualifying show. And 2 points for a Best of Show. In the case of multiple winners at the same show for a single ad or campaign, the maximum points that can be awarded is two (or three if one is a Best of Show).

"Ad Points", in order to achieve more separation and spread, are basically double. 2 for a winner. 4 for a Best of Show. 1 point each for a second or third winner for the same ad in the same show. And 3 points for a Cannes Gold, a One Show Gold or a D&AD Silver.

Finally, in the case of Tables One and Two (Commercials and Print Ads), we've applied a tie-break when points scored are equal. This is based on a combination of wins in depth (difficulty shows/level awards) and wins in breadth (# of shows and regions). We don't do tie-breakers in the top 5 in these Tables or in Tables 3 to 8, where the number of points is larger and both (or more) parties deserve to share the higher ranking.

(* TV winners vs Print winners – a comment: the problem is not just more print than TV winners in total at the same show, but also more "multiple wins" in print for the same work.

At Cannes, for example, (and where Cannes leads others follow) in TV, a worthy entry can win a Lion as a single or in a campaign (the jury can combine entries and award them as a campaign) but not as both. Even The Grand Prix doesn't get a Gold Lion too, though it will have been voted one on its way to being chosen Grand Prix.

But in Print, the same work can not just win Lions as singles and as a campaign, but also for Press and then again for Poster.

Our existing policy regarding "multiple winners" (see third and second last paragraphs above) contains the problem to some degree.

Learn to lead from those

www.berlin-school-of-creative-leadership.com

**BERLIN
SCHOOL OF
CREATIVE
LEADERSHIP**
AT STEINBEIS UNIVERSITY

THE INTERNATIONAL ADC INSTITUTE

who lead.

THE GUNN REPORT

The Showreel of The Year

2005

Presenting the 100 most awarded Commercials and Campaigns in the world in the year that was

THE SHOWREEL OF THE YEAR 2005

The 100 Most Awarded Commercials & Campaigns Worldwide in 2005.

A very warm welcome to the seventh annual edition of The Gunn Report's Showreel of The Year, which is produced and presented in association with FlaxmanWilkie.

The job of this Showreel is to provide our industry (the advertising, marketing and production communities everywhere) with the definitive screening and reference reel of the world's best commercials of the year.

Selection is based, not on the opinions of a few individuals, nor upon the choices of a single jury, but on the consensus judgement – as tallied and tabulated for The Gunn Report – of the juries serving at the world's 34 most important TV & Cinema award contests of 2005. Thus upon the totality of the votes and decisions of nearly 500 of the top advertising men and women of our day, all around the world.

As you'll notice, there are actually 105 selections on our 2005 reel. Four of this year's biggest winners (adidas "Laila", the Canadian Short Film Festival campaign, Lynx 24-7 "Getting Dressed" and Peugeot 407 "Toys") were on our 2004 reel. In addition, one of the 8th-place-in-table Orange "Don't Ruin The Movie" spots was also on last year. We wanted to give you 100 totally new selections – so these five are all repeated, but as "bonuses".

We have also, in the case of #'s 97 a & b, DFT/Department for Transportation "Lucky" and "Crash", taken the considerable liberty of "combining" commercials for the same Advertiser but from different Agencies (they might not be very pleased) – in order to cram on as much great stuff as we can. And, since campaigns are generously represented, there is a final total of 167 commercials on your reel.

Emma and Mike (that's FlaxmanWilkie) and I hope that you'll have as much fun and inspiration viewing your 2005 Showreel and sharing it with your colleagues as the three of us had putting it together for you.

Donald Gunn

1   **SMIRNOFF** • Diamond   Great Britain

A man, who dies from choking on a peanut, narrates from the afterlife what happens to his ashes. His brother, Morton, transports the urn from the church to "Live On", a swanky space age cryogenics institute – "they do some amazing things with carbon". In the deceased's case – after considerable rinsing, sluicing, sifting and refining – he ends up as a diamond. Which Morton takes to a pawn shop and ends up in a beautiful black girl's front tooth. Smirnoff "Ten times filtered".

JWT London
CD: Nick Bell
CW: Jonathan Budds
AD: Anita Davis
AP: Denise Connell

Partizan, London
Dir: Traktor
Prod: Traktor

2   **FERNET CINZANO** • Statistic   Argentina

A group of lads are hanging out and drinking Fernet Cinzano. One reads from the newspaper, "Hey, guys, check this out. One out of 10 Argentinean men is gay". There are 10 of them in the room. One hides his pink socks, one uncrosses legs, one adjusts his grip on glass to something more manly, one surreptitiously removes an earring. Etc. The only guy who hasn't heard comes back rolling an ice cube in his mouth, and reacts to the awkward silence: "What's up. Do you guys like me?" Fernet Cinzano.

Craverolanis, Buenos Aires
CD: Juan Cravero / Dario Lanis
CW: Ariel Serkin / Juan Pablo Lufrano / Toto Marelli
AD: Ariel Serkin / Juan Pablo Lufrano / Toto Marelli
AP: Tano Volpe / Pablo Gagni

Argentina Cine, Buenos Aires
Dir: Augusto Gimenez Zapiola
Prod: Pompi Huarte

3   SAN MIGUEL/REINA BEER • Carnival   Spain

Opens at the Reina Brewery (in Candelara, Canary Islands). We see a fork lift truck driver in a moose costume. Other workers are dressed up as chickens, aliens, monsters etc. Except one worker who wears normal green overalls. He is called to office by boss, who sports a Carmen Miranda turban of tropical fruits and a bare midriffed flamenco dress. His superior shares two beers and a fatherly chat and sends him home to change. Reina. Official beer of the Santa Cruz Carnival.

Arnold Worldwide Spain, Barcelona
CD: Julio Wallovits

Bus, Madrid
Dir: Juan Flesca
Prod: Marta Delgado

4a   GUINNESS EXTRA COLD • Surfer   Great Britain

Guinness "Surfer" stands as one of the greatest commercials of all-time (and winner in Table One in The Gunn Report 2000). We're on the same beach, with the same pounding bass soundtrack and the same "tick follows tock follows tick…" voiceover, as the surfers, who've been waiting, run for their boards and race for the ocean. However this time the water is freezing cold. The surfers turn around and run back out again. "It's Guinness. But Extra Cold".

Abbott Mead Vickers.BBDO, London
CD: Paul Belford / Nigel Roberts
CW: Mark Fairbanks / Markham Smith
AD: Mark Fairbanks
AP   Anita Sasdy

Exposure Films, London
Dir: J J Keith
Prod: Simon Monhemius

4b GUINNESS EXTRA COLD • Anticipation   Great Britain

Another classic Guinness commercial was "Anticipation".
Because the perfect pint of Guinness takes 119.5 seconds
to pour - under the theme "Good things come to those
who wait" - we saw an angular bloke performing
a frenetic and somewhat eccentric dance around his pint
glass as it is slowly filled. (The quirky music became a big
hit in clubs). In this version, however, the dance is
performed by an Eskimo in furs. (Another adland in-joke:
"Eskimo" was an award-winning Extra Cold print ad).
"It's Guinness. But Extra Cold".

Abbott Mead Vickers.BBDO, London
CD: Paul Belford / Nigel Roberts
CW: Mark Fairbanks / Markham Smith
AD: Mark Fairbanks
AP: Anita Sasdy

Exposure Films, London
Dir: J J Keith
Prod: Simon Monhemius

4c GUINNESS EXTRA COLD • Snail   Great Britain

"Bet on Black" (third in Table One in The Gunn Report
2000) was one of the all-time great Guinness
commercials, featuring frenzied Cuban gamblers at
an illicit snail race. We open on the winning snail from
the original ad at the starting line yet again. However
this time round the miserable mollusc is shaking and
shivering with cold. He sneezes and swiftly retreats.
"It's Guinness. But Extra Cold".

Abbott Mead Vickers.BBDO, London
CD: Paul Belford / Nigel Roberts
CW: Mark Fairbanks / Markham Smith
AD: Mark Fairbanks
AP: Anita Sasdy

Exposure Films, London
Dir: J J Keith
Prod: Simon Monhemius

5a **MOUNTAIN DEW** • Hallway   USA

The "Spy vs. Spy" cartoon characters, who have perpetrated dastardly deeds on each other since the 60's in the pages of Mad Magazine, are the protagonists in the Mountain Dew campaign. In "Hallway", white spy leaves a booby-trap with a can of Mountain Dew as bait outside the Spy Inc. office. Black spy rightly suspects a mallet awaits to clobber him from above. He jams a pencil in it. But the Dew sits on a sprung trap which propels black spy into the mallet. Do The Dew.

BBDO, New York
CD: Bill Bruce
CW: Bill Bruce
AD: Doris Cassar
AP: Hyatt Choate

Partizan, Los Angeles
Dir: Traktor
Prod: Traktor

5b **MOUNTAIN DEW** • Helicopter   USA

Based on Mad Magazine's "Spy vs. Spy" strip, white spy lures black spy to a certain street corner with a strategically placed Mountain Dew machine. He hovers above in a helicopter and clobbers his enemy with a boxing glove on a spring. But the recoil clobbers him too. One up to black spy who puts his coin in for a Dew. The spring-loaded pavement smashes him into the wall. Do The Dew.

BBDO, New York
CD: Bill Bruce
CW: Bill Bruce
AD: Doris Cassar
AP: Hyatt Choate

Partizan, Los Angeles
Dir: Traktor
Prod: Traktor

5c   **MOUNTAIN DEW** • Canopy   USA

White spy (as in "Spy vs. Spy" strip in Mad Magazine) arrives to burglarise the Spy Inc. office. But black spy escapes in the elevator with a can of Mountain Dew. White spy hears elevator leave so he tiptoes to the Mountain Dew machine. A trapdoor awaits and he hurtles down a chute and out of the building. He falls 10 storeys and through a canopy landing in a heap on black spy's head. Do The Dew.

BBDO, New York
CD: Bill Bruce
CW: Bill Bruce
AD: Doris Cassar
AP: Hyatt Choate

Partizan, Los Angeles
Dir: Traktor
Prod: Traktor

6   **COCA-COLA** • Rivalries   49th   Argentina

Comical claymation pairings of natural enemies are shown. A fly swat and a buzzing insect. A woodcutter and a tree. A housewife about to chop a plucked chicken's head off. A hippy and a bar of soap. Etc. All have TV or radio on with a big soccer match. Suddenly: "Goooall!" "The enemies all embrace, hug, rejoice and dance around together. Even a chap in bedroom with wife's lover who emerges from the wardrobe. "Only the national team can bind us this way". Coca Cola.

Santo, Buenos Aires
CD: Sebastian Wilhelm / Maximiliano Anselmo
CW: Sebastian Wilhelm
AD: Maximiliano Anselmo

Vinton Studios, Portland, OR
Dir: Mark Gustafson
Prod: Lourri Hammock

7a K-FEE CAFFEINE DRINK • Car   Germany

(These 20 seconders apparently got massive, spontaneous viral exposure even before they ran on air). Soft music under, as we see a car driving up an idyllic, winding mountain road. The day is beautiful, the meadows and trees are the lushest green. Suddenly an ugly beast jumps into the frame in foreground, screaming wildly. Title: "Ever been so wide awake?" SFX: rapid heart beat. Pack shot with pulsing can. K-Fee. Canned caffeine with coffee.

Jung von Matt Germany, Hamburg
CD: Constantin Kaloff / Ove Gley
CW: Daniel Frericks / Eskil Puhl
AD: Frank Aldorf
AP: Mark Rota

Cobblestone Filmproduktion, Hamburg
Dir: Kai Sehr
Prod: Kai Stoecker

7b K-FEE CAFFEINE DRINK • Golf   Germany

We open on a lovely day out on a lovely golf course (it could be in Florida). Trees in foreground, lake in background, soft chirping of crickets. A golfer on a green takes his putt. Suddenly a ghoulish head jumps onto screen – both upside down and screaming wildly. Title: "Ever been so wide awake?" SFX: thumping heartbeat. K-Fee pack shot with pulsing can. K-Fee Caffeine with coffee.

Jung von Matt Germany, Hamburg
CD: Constantin Kaloff / Ove Gley
CW: Daniel Frericks / Eskil Puhl
AD: Frank Aldorf
AP: Mark Rota

Cobblestone Filmproduktion, Hamburg
Dir: Kai Sehr
Prod: Kai Stoecker

7c K-FEE CAFFEINE DRINK • Beach   Germany

A beautiful sunset on a lovely beach. Serene love song under. A young couple slowly approach each other across the golden sand. Coy glances, he gently takes her hand. But just before they kiss, a monstrous head jumps into frame on foreground – screaming wildly. (Shades of Edvard Munch). Title on black: "Ever been so wide awake?" SFX : thumping heartbeat. K-Fee. Caffeine with coffee.

Jung von Matt Germany, Hamburg
CD: Constantin Kaloff / Ove Gley
CW: Daniel Frericks / Eskil Puhl
AD: Frank Aldorf
AP: Mark Rota

Cobblestone Filmproduktion, Hamburg
Dir: Kai Sehr
Prod: Kai Stoecker

8 PEPSI • Surf   Brazil

The world's finest footballers are chilling out on a tropical beach. Two surfers roll up, point to the "Surfers Only" sign and kick the players' ball out to sea. Becks, Roberto Carlos, Ronaldinho, Raul, Van der Waart, Fernando Torres and co. exchange a look, then grab surf boards and hit the waves for an amazing display of overhead kicks, thudding headers and fearsome volleys as they board hither and thither in the pounding surf. And thanks to Thierry Henry's vigilance, the surfers are denied access to their Pepsi cooler. Pepsi.

AlmapBBDO, Sao Paulo
CD: Marcello Serpa
CW: Dulcidio Caldeira
AD: Marcello Serpa / Cesar Finamori
AP: Pierre Marcus

@radical.media, London
Dir: Tarsem Singh

9 CALIFORNIA MILK PROCESSOR BOARD • Russian Family | 44th | USA

Dirgeful music under as a Russian family (Dad, Mum, 2 kids and Babooshka) huddle over dinner (which looks like watery soup) in their modest flatlet. Suddenly a perky little voice is heard: "Ho! Ho! How about some fresh baked cookies". It's the Pillsbury Doughboy with a plateful. Music changes to joyful. Family dance round table feeding each other chocolate chip cookies. Then a shriek from the kitchen. Music stops. Mom appears shaking an empty milk carton. Dirgeful music resumes. "Got Milk?"

Goodby Silverstein & Partners, San Francisco
CD: Jeff Goodby
CW: Tyler McKellar
AD: Stefan Copiz
AP: Tod Puckett

Biscuit Filmworks, Los Angeles
Dir: Noam Murro
Prod: Jay Shapiro

10 CHARAL BEEF • The Race | 30th | France

Opens - like in thousands of wildlife documentaries - on a cheetah, the fastest of land carnivores, chasing an antelope across savannah plain. Suddenly a man sprints into frame, overtakes the cheetah, scoops up the antelope and races away. The cheetah slows to a halt looking duly pissed off and puzzled. Title over "Guess who's the biggest carnivore?" Cut to Charal logo and their fork scratch mnemonic. "The best meat".

Leo Burnett Paris, Boulogne-Billancourt
CD: Antoine Barthuel / Daniel Fohr
CW: Jean-François Goize
AD: Stephan Ferens
AP: Catherine Guiol

Quad Productions, Paris
Dir: Rémy Belvaux

11   MARMITE • The Blob   Great Britain

An affectionate 50's B-movie spoof: small town America, shoppers shriek and scatter as a monstrous dark brown "Blob" emerges from the supermarket and trundles ominously down the High Street. A hammed-up horror soundtrack accompanies. Townsfolk take cover, shop-keepers barricade their premises. But while some scramble away in fear, others seem strangely drawn to "The Blob" and start to run forward and dive into it. Marmite. "You either love it or hate it".

DDB London
CW: Sam Oliver
AD: Shishir Patel
AP: Lucinda Ker

The Sweet Shop, Auckland
Dir: Steve Ayson
Prod: Tony Whyman

12   AUSTRALIAN MEAT & LIVESTOCK COMMISSION • Unaustralian   Australia

A middle-aged bloke sits before an Australian flag (like in a party political broadcast) and lambasts "the creeping tide of unaustralianism eroding our great traditions". A balanced Australia Day diet, he maintains, should consist of a few juicy lamb chops and beer. He castigates the alternatives favoured by pot-smoking, hippy vegetarians. "Do they think the diggers in the trenches were fighting for tofu sausages?" "So don't be unaustralian. Serve lamb on Australia Day. You know it makes sense".

BMF Advertising, Sydney
CD: Warren Brown
CW: Dennis Koutoulogenis
AD: Dale McGuinness
AP: Tamyson Power

2 Feet Films, Sydney
Dir: Phil Rich
Prod: Phil Rich

13a ALTOIDS SOURS • People of Pain — USA

British anthropologist, Sir Gerald Pines, introduces us to Altoidia, "Land of sour. People of pain", whose inhabitants are rendered immune to pain by prolonged exposure to Altoids Sours. The odd arrow in the bottom or machete in the skull will pass unnoticed and their "simple greetings" consist of a mutual groin kick. After months of study, comes the day of Sir Gerald's initiation: he is catapulted through the air to land on a campfire. Explore sours at altoidia.com.

Leo Burnett, Chicago

CD: Noel Haan / G. Andrew Meyer
CW: G Andrew Meyer
AD: Noel Haan
AP: Vincent Geraghty / David Moore

MJZ, Los Angeles

Prod: Deb Tietjen

13b ALTOIDS SOURS • Mastering the Mother Tongue — USA

Sir Gerald Pines, intrepid anthropologist, is researching the unique language of the mythical island of Altoidia- "Sucky-Sucky". When a native offers him gum, he tries the mother tongue himself, inadvertently saying, "Your mother smells like monkey butt". The offended tribesmen release a trap, propelling Sir Gerald skywards and leaving him dangling from a palm tree. "Hello! Something I said?" Explore sours at altoidia.com.

Leo Burnett, Chicago

CD: Noel Haan / G. Andrew Meyer
CW: G Andrew Meyer
AD: Noel Haan
AP: Vincent Geraghty / David Moore

MJZ, Los Angeles

Prod: Deb Tietjen

13c **ALTOIDS SOURS** • Fable of the Fruit Bat   USA

In Altoidia, anthropologist and documentary filmmaker Sir Gerald Pines interviews the tribal chief about their legendary fruit bat – "a wing-ed giant driven mad by the slightest hint of sours". The explorer is inclined to debunk the fable of the fruit bat, until a prime specimen of the mythical beast swoops from the sky, scoops him up – "Bad doggie, bad doggie" - and drops him with a comic thud on a Land Rover. Explore sours at altoidia.com.

Leo Burnett, Chicago
CD: Noel Haan / G. Andrew Meyer
CW: G Andrew Meyer
AD: Noel Haan
AP: Vincent Geraghty / David Moore

MJZ, Los Angeles
Prod: Deb Tietjen

14 **KIMS CRISPS** • Mix Up   Norway

A guy gets home with a grocery bag – "Anything happen yet?" he asks pal who's settling in for match on telly. Dip is ready on table and he reaches in bag for the Kims Crisps he's bought… and pulls out a lettuce. There's also a bunch of radishes and other healthsome veggies. Realising he's picked up wrong bag, they both start screaming. Cut to a couple of svelte, modelly lads at their place, finding Kims Crisps in their grocery bag and also screaming, or in their case shrieking. No Kims. No Joy.

Try Advertising Agency, Oslo
CW: Tore Woll
AD: Erlend Klouman Høiner
AP: Cathrine Wennersten

Motion Blur, Oslo
Dir: Harald Zwart
Prod: Espen Horn

15a SKITTLES GUM • Shelter   Great Britain

An outwards bound expert shows us how to build a survival shelter. "The best thing is you can find everything you want right here in the woods". He piles bracken and pulls a roof of woven branches over his pit. It's protected from wind being below surface level he explains, and will keep us snug and warm. Plus, "You could have a wank in there. No one would see you". He removes the gum from his mouth and sticks it on the pack. Title: "Me and my fruity mouth".

TBWA\London
CD: Trevor Beattie
CW: Alasdair Graham
AD: Frazer Jelleyman
AP: Kate Hitchings

Independent Films, London
Dir: Tim Godsall
Prod: Fergus Brown

15b SKITTLES GUM • Cherubs   Great Britain

An erudite and ascetic art historian tells us about a baroque painting in a gallery, "The Return of the Etruscan Women". He points out how the artist "uses the divine proportion to incorporate geometric anomalies which hint to us thinly veiled symbolism within the work". It also features, "mythological entities such as these cherubs, who appear to be bumming each other". He apologies and removes the gum from his mouth and sticks it on the pack. Title: "Me and my fruity mouth".

TBWA\London
CD: Trevor Beattie
CW: Alasdair Graham
AD: Frazer Jelleyman
AP: Kate Hitchings

Independent Films, London
Dir: Tim Godsall
Prod: Fergus Brown

16 ENERGISER BATTERIES • Mano Japonesa   24th   USA

A man who lost an arm in an accident receives an implant from a Japanese donor. Now he can't stop taking photos with his digital camera. We see him snapping away… the guy next to him in a urinal, all of his family from every possible angle at a birthday party, man in row in front in a movie, his long-suffering wife throughout the night in bed. Luckily he uses Energiser e2 Lithium – "The longest lasting batteries in a digital camera". Keep going.

Grupo Gallegos, Long Beach
CD: Favio Ucedo
CW: Aida Roman / Martin Jalfen
AD: Facundo Romero

Flip Films, Santa Monica
Dir: Nicolas Kasakoff
Prod: Adrian Castagna

17 POLIFLOR FURNITURE POLISH • Wind   Brazil

A TV set and a household fan sit side by side on top of a nice-looking, wooden chest of drawers. The fan rotates slowly through 90°. As it turns towards the TV, it blows it across the surface. The second time the fan turns that way, the TV set slides off the chest of drawers with a crash. Super: "The best furniture cream". Poliflor. From Reckitt Benckiser.

JWT, Sao Paulo
CD: A Francucci / A Soares / F Nobre / J Linneu
CW: Romero Cavalcanti
AD: Claudia Fugita
AP: Anna Bohm

Jodaf Mixer, Sao Paulo
Dir: Joao Daniel Tikhomiroff
Prod: Veronica Rodivicius

18 SHOWBOUND NATURALS • Ping Pong — USA

In games room at home a man is playing table tennis. He's pretty good – and so evidently is his opponent, as all the guy's forehand and backhand smashes are returned with equal ferocity. It's a really long rally. Cut to reverse shot – opponent must be rather short as we can't see him, only bat operating at just above table level. The next shot reveals the ping pong bat is strapped to a dog's tail, which is wagging vigorously as he tucks into a bowl of Showbound Naturals. "You can't make a dog happier."

Grey Worldwide, New York
CD: Jonathan Rodgers / Tim Mellors
CW: Jonathan Rodgers
AD: Steve Krauss
AP: Diana Gay

HKM Productions, Hollywood
Dir: Nelson Cabrerra
Prod: Carl Swan

19 WHISKAS CAT FOOD • Scratches — Brazil

A guy in an elevator arriving at work has a scratch on his neck. Colleagues notice and smirk. A slow, sexy, raspy song plays under as he crosses the open plan office. His co workers, a secretary who seems a little aroused, envious guys sniggering at the coffee machine, etc, all see the scratch as evidence of a night of wild sex. Wrong. Cut to title: "Don't forget. Cats prefer Whiskas". Ends on our hero, that night, feeding his kitty what she prefers.

AlmapBBDO, Sao Paulo
CD: Marcello Serpa / Cassio Zanatta / Giba Lages
CW: Cassio Zanatta
AD: Giba Lages / Jose Carlos Lollo
AP: Egisto Betti

Jodaf Mixer, Sao Paulo
Dir: Michel Tikhomiroff

20a **AXE BODY SPRAY** • Residue — USA

Opens on a glamorous secretary sensuously stroking a silvery office stapler. A girl in a hardware store caresses nuts and bolts. A woman in a kitchen rubs her bottom with a frying pan. A girl embraces a bunch of tin foil. Further women are nearly having sex with a metal step ladder… with a toaster in an appliance store, etc. All is explained when we see a guy, who's got the last spray from his Axe canister, discard it in a recycling bin. New Longer Lasting Axe Effect.

Bartle Bogle Hegarty, New York
CD: William Gelner
CW: Matt Ian / Brian Friedrich
AD: Amee Shah
AP: Stacey Higgins

Biscuit Filmworks, Los Angeles
Dir: Noam Murro
Prod: Shawn Lacey Tessaro

20b **AXE SHOWER GEL** • Bath — USA

SFX: splish, splash, as we open on attractive young woman kneeling in front of a bathtub, giving someone a bath. Because of camera position, we cannot see the occupant. She coos in baby talk, "You like bathtime don't you. We're going to get you nice and clean. Can you tell me how old you are?" "Twenty two", comes the gruff reply. "Yes you are!" say the woman admiringly. Axe Shower Gel. "How dirty boys get clean."

Bartle Bogle Hegarty, New York
CD: William Gelner
CW: Tom Kraemer
AD: Nick Klinkert
AP: Lisa Gatto

HSI Productions, New York
Dir: Joe Public
Prod: Kerstin Emhoff

20c **AXE SHOWER GEL** • Pipe USA

  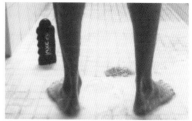

Pole dancing belongs in strip clubs. But here we see a gorgeous blonde pole dancing with an exposed pipe that runs up through her apartment. On the floor above a sexy brunette is writhing around said pipe. The woman on next storey hangs upside down on it with her thighs. Camera moves on up to top floor apartment: we see feet of a guy who's showering with Axe and the drain that goes into the pipe. Axe Shower Gel – "How dirty boys get clean".

Bartle Bogle Hegarty, New York
CD: William Gelner
CW: Matt Ian
AD: Amee Shah
AP: Lisa Gatto

HSI Productions, New York
Dir: Joe Public
Prod: Kerstin Emhoff

21 **REXONA FOR MEN** • Stunt City Great Britain

Stunt City. The one place on earth where Rexona For Men gets a proper workout. We're treated to a succession of far-fetched Hollywood stunts, as guys on their way to work in the morning dive from apartment windows to catch a bus or leap onto moving taxis or dangle from helicopter runners. And motorbikes rocket down steps, and folks are on fire, and cars do wheelies around town and smash through plate glass windows. Rexona for Men. "Over the top protection for under the arms".

Lowe, London
CD: Ed Morris
CW: Geoff Smith
AD: Simon Butler
AP: Charles Crisp

Stink, London
Dir: Ivan Zacharias
Prod: Nick Landon

22a REXONA DRY DEODORANT • Shirts   Argentina

We pass the day with a guy who sweats a lot under his arms. So what does he do? He ambushes other blokes and hijacks their shirts and T-shirts. His victims include a gent outside a mall, a taxi-driver, a hot dog seller. He even steals shirts from a balcony and appropriates an unfortunate partygoer's bear costume.
Title: "Better change the deodorant." Rexona Men's. Won't let you down.

VegaOlmosPonce, Buenos Aires
CD: Hernán Ponce / Sebastián Stagno / Rafael d'Alvia
CW: Matías Corbelle
AD: Diego Sánchez
AP: Roberto Carsillo

Revolucion, Buenos Aires
Dir: Armando Bo
Prod: Patricio Alvarez Casado

22b AXE BODY SPRAY • No   Argentina

A man sits down and whispers in the ear of a girl reading her book by the seaside. She tells him "No". Cut to the couple laughing and sharing a coffee. He leans forward and whispers. "No". They come out of a movie. She consults her watch and says "No". It's "No" again in the disco … and outside his apartment … and on the sofa. Cut to the contented couple asleep in bed with super: "It's a matter of time." "That's why Axe lasts 24 hours." Ends on girl, ruefully happy, cooking his breakfast egg. Axe.

VegaOlmosPonce, Buenos Aires
CD: Hernán Ponce / Sebastián Stagno / Rafael d'Alvia
CW: Analía Ríos
AD: Ricardo Armentano
AP: Roberto Carsillo

La Banda Films, Beverly Hills
Dir: José Pratt
Prod: Paco Cossio

23   LYNX 24/7 BODY SPRAY • Getting Dressed   4th=   Great Britain

A girl and a boy (castable as Romeo and Juliet) wake up in bed. Israel Kamakowiwoole's "Somewhere Over the Rainbow" under, as they trace their way from her bedroom, back through city, getting dressed again as they go – his trousers from over the garden gate, her shirt on a parking meter, his T-shirt on a traffic light. The boy's last shoe sits by two facing shopping trolleys in a supermarket. Lynx 24-7 works 24 hours a day. "Because you never know when."

Bartle Bogle Hegarty, London
CD: Rosie Arnold
CW: Nick Gill
AP: Amy Sugdon

Small Family Business, London
Dir: Ringan Ledwidge
Prod: Sally Humphries

24a **PAMPERS** • Stairs　　　　　　38th　Argentina

Open on an infant at home toddling towards the
staircase. His mom leaps up: "No, No". Fast forward
25 years or so to a man who won't go up an escalator
… or climb a stepladder to change a bulb … or climb
stadium stairs with a big match playing … or steps into
an aeroplane (stewardess closes door). Etc. Cut back
to opening scene and title over "Are you doing the
right thing for your child's development?" Pampers.com.
Learn more.

Del Campo Nazca Saatchi & Saatchi, Buenos Aires
CD:　　Gastón Bigio / Pablo Gil
CW:　　Gastón Bigio / Pablo Gil
AD:　　Sebastián Garín / Jonathan Gurvit
AP:　　Camilo Rojas / Adrian Aspani

Pioneer, Buenos Aires
Dir:　　Luciano Podcaminsky
Prod:　 Flora Fernandez Marengo

24b **PAMPERS** • Crying　　　　　　38th　Argentina

A toddler is playing with a toy which a second child
snatches away. Mom retrieves it, but, seeing her infant is
crying, thinks he'll learn if she doesn't give it back. Fast
forward 25 years or so to a man who screws up his face
and bawls when girl at movies takes some of his
popcorn … when hotel porter takes his suitcase … when
waiter takes his plate away … and – most surprisingly –
in bedroom when girlfriend takes his shirt off. "Are you
doing the right thing for your child's development?"
Pampers.com. Learn more.

Del Campo Nazca Saatchi & Saatchi, Buenos Aires
CD:　　Gastón Bigio / Pablo Gil
CW:　　Gastón Bigio / Pablo Gil
AD:　　Sebastián Garín / Jonathan Gurvit
AP:　　Camilo Rojas / Adrian Aspani

Pioneer, Buenos Aires
Dir:　　Luciano Podcaminsky
Prod:　 Flora Fernandez Marengo

25 SCOTCH ESSENCE OF CHICKEN • Date — Thailand

A young couple sit across a table from each other in a restaurant. The girl looks depressed. She tells her boyfriend not to work so hard – "You don't have time for us," she gently remonstrates. He puts his hand over hers. Next we know he's tapping his finger on her hand and moving it around like a computer mouse. He even picks it up to give rub at the roller and gives it a couple of sharp knocks on the table. Scotch Essence of Chicken. Suitable for workaholics.

Y&R Thailand, Bangkok
CD: Piya Boontarig
CW: Piya Boontarig / Penporn Somnus
AD: Penporn Somnus
AP: Piya Boontarig

Phenomena, Bangkok
Dir: Thanonchai Sornsrivichai

26a VIAGRA • Golf — Canada

A golfer drops an amazing putt. His opponent, "Wow! Can you believe that!" Golfer (an Onassis lookalike), "Hey, that's nothing. This morning I…" a metallic censorship tone drowns out what he is telling his friend, and a Viagra logo appears over his mouth. End on opponent chuckling in admiration as he lines up his own putt. Talk to your Doctor. Viagra.

Taxi, Toronto
CD: Zak Mroueh / Lance Martin
CW: Irfan Khan
AD: Ron Smrczek
AP: Jennifer Mete

The Partners' Film Company, Toronto
Dir: Joachim Back
Prod: Gigi Realini / Link York

26b VIAGRA • Office — Canada

Opens on two men and a woman in the office kitchen. One guy greets the other, "Hey, Tom, you're lookin' good. You been working out?" Tom, "No, but I've been…" A metallic censorship tone drowns out whatever he is recounting, while a Viagra logo appears over his mouth. The woman co-worker gives a nervous laugh and toasts him with her coffee mug – "Bravo". Talk to your Doctor. Viagra.

Taxi, Toronto
CD: Zak Mroueh / Lance Martin
CW: Irfan Khan
AD: Ron Smrczek
AP: Jennifer Mete

The Partners' Film Company, Toronto
Dir: Joachim Back
Prod: Gigi Realini / Link York

26c VIAGRA • Coach — Canada

A sports coach is at lectern at a press conference. "How do you feel about retirement?" "Pretty darn good. Next". A woman reporter stands, "What are you going to do with all your free time?" Coach, "Well, I'm gonna spend a little more time…" Metallic censorship tone replaces what he's saying, while a Viagra logo appears over his mouth. The reporter sits down with a little smile. Coach, "Next". Talk to your Doctor. Viagra.

Taxi, Toronto
CD: Zak Mroueh / Lance Martin
CW: Irfan Khan
AD: Ron Smrczek
AP: Jennifer Mete

The Partners' Film Company, Toronto
Dir: Joachim Back
Prod: Gigi Realini / Link York

27 LEVI'S 501's WITH ANTI-FIT • Midsummer   Great Britain

Act III, Scene 1 of "A Midsummer Night's Dream" in the streets of modern L.A. A young man is jostled by a Latino gang who mock the shape of his Levi's. Quoting Bottom's lines, when he wakes with an ass's head, he sees them off, while down the road in a diner a beautiful waitress, as Titania, catches the cut of his denim: "What angel wakes me from my flowery bed?" The couple fall hopelessly in love. Levi's 501. Jeans with Anti-Fit.

Bartle Bogle Hegarty, London
CD: Marc Shillum
CW: Nick Gill
AD: Nick Gill
AP: Bradly Woodus

Independent Films, London / Biscuit Filmworks, Los Angeles
Dir: Noam Murro

28a ADIDAS • Unstoppable   19th   USA

Tracy McGrady is a scoring machine. He is nearly impossible to stop, even for the NBA's best defenders. Here "T Mac" is featured in a Gulliver's Travels-type encounter with a veritable army of miniature helicopters, trucks, paratroopers and ground-to-air missile launchers who deploy their weaponry in an attempt to halt his progress down the court. Tracy completes a spectacular slam-dunk and runs back to the free throw line. Impossible Is Nothing. adidas.

TBWA\Chiat\Day (180\TBWA), San Francisco
CD: Chuck McBride / Geoff Edwards / Scott Duchon
CW: Scott Duchon
AD: Geoff Edwards
AP: Jennifer Golub / Andrea Bustabade

Smuggler, Los Angeles
Dir: Brian Beletec

28b **ADIDAS** • Improvisation — USA

Basketball mega-star, Chauncey Billups, stalks onto an empty court. Horror movie soundtrack under. As Chauncey starts his run, the court itself comes to life proving to be the ultimate opponent. The parquet tiles rise from the floor to block him, and ripple up into an enormous wooden wave. Billups bounds straight through the engulfing barrier, leaps, shoots and scores a perfect three-pointer. Impossible Is Nothing. adidas.

TBWA\Chiat\Day (180\TBWA), San Francisco
CD: Chuck McBride
CW: Scott Duchon / Joe Rose
AD: Geoff Edwards / Brandon Mugar / Marco Warsham
AP: Jennifer Golub / Andrea Bustabade

RSA USA, New York
Dir: Jake Scott
Prod: Jules Daly / Fran McGivern

28c **ADIDAS** • Carry — 41st — USA

The NBA's reigning MVP, Kevin Garnett, is the consummate leader – a player who can "put people on his back" to overcome anything. In this spot, with "I got the whole world in my hands" playing under, he literally does so. As he walks the streets of LA, a whole mountain of people (teammates, family, friends) pile onto his shoulders (some abandon cars or exit buses, some jump from rooftops) to create a precarious, teetering human tower. Impossible Is Nothing. adidas.

TBWA\Chiat\Day (180\TBWA), San Francisco
CD: Chuck McBride
CW: Scott Duchon / Joe Rose
AD: Geoff Edwards / Brandon Mugar / Marco Warsham

Biscuit Filmworks, Los Angeles
Dir: Noam Murro

29 DIESEL JEANS • Kaboom! — The Netherlands

A cartoon vision of war shot with the most eccentric, economy props. A collection of plant pots and salt and pepper shakers represent a city. Radar warning sounds. A toy blue plastic plane is on the way – its rockets are matchsticks. With much "Boom, boom! Ack! Ack! Kerpow!" –ing, ground-to-air missiles (sticks with clown heads) are launched. A bomber follows in and drops its peanuts. Christmas tree balls represent the rubble in the devastated metropolis below. Diesel. For Successful Living.

Kesselskramer, Amsterdam
CD: Dave Bell
CW: Dave Bell
AD: Karen Heuter

Czar.us, New York
Dir: Pes
Prod: Steve Shore

30 RAINHA TRAINERS • Underwear — Brazil

Opens at dawn in the streets of Sao Paulo. A man comes sprinting round a corner in just his Y-fronts and his trainers. Next shot shows a man in a suit and panting, apparently chasing after the first man. Intercut between the two men, the Rainha trainers and spectators like a pair or early schoolgirls, a kiosk holder opening up. Then we see the man in underpants catch up with and overtake his rival. VO: "And now he's three laps up on the betrayed husband." Close with Rainha logo.

F/Nazca Saatchi & Saatchi, Sao Paulo
CD: Fábio Fernandes
CW: Fábio Fernandes / Eduardo Lima
AD: Luciano Lincoln
AP: Regiani Petinelli

Cia de Cinema, Sao Paulo
Dir: Claudio Borrelli
Prod: Germano Jr.

31 H&M STORES/KARL LAGERFELD COLLECTION • Karl Lagerfeld 37th Sweden

Shot in black and white and reminiscent of Fellini, two queeny old gents from the Paris fashion world discuss what seems to be a huge scandal. Lurid cutaways show betrayed society matrons emptying wardrobes, throwing tantrums, whipping servants – the question on everyone's outraged lips: "Is it true?" Finally Karl Lagerfeld himself confirms it and responds: "Cheap. What a depressing word. It's all about taste. If you're cheap, nothing helps". Karl Lagerfeld Collection at H&M.

Red Room, Stockholm
CD: Jan Nord
CW: Jan Nord / Johan Renck
AD: Jan Nord / Johan Renck

RAF, Stockholm
Dir: Johan Renck
Prod: Anna Gustafsson

32a NIKE • Scary House USA

Two kids creep through the fence to the scary house at the end of a street. Boy goads his little sister to ring the bell. She shrieks in horror at what comes to the door. And transforms into Marion Jones (the fastest woman in the world) in her white Nike Swift suit. Marion, still screaming, races through town (Savannah, Georgia, incidentally – said to be the most haunted city in the USA) to the safety of home. Where she becomes the little girl again. "You're faster than you think". Nikespeed.com.

Wieden+Kennedy, Portland, OR
CD: Hal Curtis / Mike Byrne
CW: Alberto Ponte
AD: Bill Karow
AP: Ben Grylewicz / Andrew Loevenguth

Partizan, Los Angeles
Dir: Traktor
Prod: Traktor

32b **NIKE** • Tennis Instructor USA

The females at the tennis club giggle, preen and fix their make-up as the blonde Adonis of a coach arrives for the day in his white convertible. He ponces around with his clipboard as the lesson gets under way. The instructor does a double take however, when young girl serving becomes… Serena Williams. As does another performing a forehand smash… and one diving for a net return… soon Serenas are playing on all the courts. "You're faster than you think". Nikespeed.com.

Wieden+Kennedy, Portland, OR
CD: Hal Curtis / Mike Byrne
CW: Alberto Ponte
AD: Bill Karow
AP: Andrew Loevenguth

Gorgeous Enterprises, London
Dir: Chris Palmer
Prod: Rupert Smythe

33 **VOLKSWAGEN GOLF DSG** • Kids on Steps 6th Germany

Two boys are sitting on the steps outside a house, with hands outstretched, making "vroom, vroom" noises, playing at driving. While one boy changes gear and makes engine noises accordingly, the other lad just goes on without a break, his pitch becoming higher in smooth transitions. Cut to Mum closing window. Cut to family car in driveway – a Golf DSG. Cut back to kid still going on, now beetroot coloured. "Shifts gears without interruption". The Golf with Direct Shift Gearbox.

DDB Germany, Berlin
CD: Amir Kassaei / Wolfgang Schneider /
     Mathias Stiller
CW: Nico Akkermann / Vinny Warren
AD: Bart Kooij / Scott Smith
AP: Marion Lange

Cobblestone Filmproduktion, Hamburg
Dir: Sebastian Strasser
Prod: Pieter Lony

34 **CITROEN C4** • Carbot 10th Great Britain

Opens on a silver C4 in a car park somewhere. This new Citroen bristles with so much electronic wizardry that it can't help coming to life. To a thumping number from the group Rythmes Digitales, the car opens up and transforms itself into a dancing robot with all the cheesiest disco and break dancing (or should it be brake dancing?) moves. The new Citroen C4. Alive With Technology.

Euro RSCG London
CD: Justin Hooper
CW: Matthew Anderson / Steven Nicholls
AD: Matthew Anderson / Steven Nicholls
AP: Nicola Tucker

Spy Films, Toronto
Dir: Neill Blomkamp
Prod: Winston Helgason / Carlo Trulli

35 FORD RANGER OPEN CAB · King Kong · 16th · Thailand

A man has stopped at the roadside for a call of nature. A giant monkey hand snatches his banana-laden truck. It's a young gorilla. He plays at banging the truck against a rock. He gets a clip in the ear from Dad who tells him to eat his lunch (the banana load). Kid defiantly plays on. Dad confiscates truck. Kid bawls. Dad contemplates truck with respect, then flips it away. For it to land again behind owner, just buttoning his jeans. "In a man's world, you must be tough". Ford Ranger Open Cab.

JWT Bangkok
CD: Pinit Chantaprateep
CW: Wichian Thongsuksiri
AD: Rungsun Suwannachitra / Taya Soonthonvipat

Phenomena, Bangkok
Dir: Thanonchai Sornsrivichai
Prod: Piyawan Mungkung

36 VOLKSWAGEN GOLF GTI · Policemen · Mexico

A police car is parked in a leafy suburb – the cops inside are having a coffee. Controller on radio: "Attention all units. We have a 40 in progress. Bross Jewellers Centre. Suspects heading to Main and Uruguay Streets." Cops down their coffees, belt up, hats on, gun engine. Controller: "They are driving a red Golf GTI". Cops switch off motor, remove hats, unbuckle, drink more coffee. VW Logo. Golf 180hp.

DDB Mexico, Mexico City
CD: Sebastian Arrechedera / Yosu Aranguena / Martin Campo
CW: Yosu Aranguena
AD: Martin Campo
AP: Alejandro Fernandez

Garcia Bross y Asociados, Mexico City
Dir: Simon Bross
Prod: Alberto Bross

37   **VOLKSWAGEN GOLF GTI** • Hypnotist   Singapore

In a smoky cocktail lounge a group of volunteers stand on stage hypnotised. The hypnotist announces: "When I say the word 'Awake' you will find the city hit by an earthquake". He snaps his fingers – "Awake!" The subjects on stage scurry hither and thither taking cover, cower behind chairs, hug each other. Except one woman, who dashes from the stage and escapes through the back door to take refuge in her car. The new Golf. Awarded 5 stars for occupant protection. VW logo. "Engineered Inside Out".

Fallon Singapore
CD: Calvin Soh / Yang Yeo
CW: Calvin Soh / Craig Howie
AD: David Seah / Aaron Phua
AP: Gwynn Wong

Stink, London
Dir: Laurence Hamburger
Prod: Daniel Bergman / Sally Llewellyn

38   **VOLKSWAGEN GOLF GTI** • Singin' In The Rain   Great Britain

We open on Gene Kelly and his immortal dance number from "Singing in The Rain". But as he closes his umbrella down and hands it to a passer-by, things become different. The soundtrack acquires a breakbeat and Kelly's classic steps – down slick sidewalks, splashing through puddles, swinging round a lamp-post - are updated into a body-popping, break-dancing routine. He comes to a halt at last to admire a car parked by the pavement. A cop in uniform looks on too. The new Golf GTI. The original, updated.

DDB London
CD: Martin Loraine
CW: Martin Loraine
AD: Steve Jones

Stink, London
Dir: Jake Knight / Ryoko Tanaka

39 **TOYOTA PRIUS** • Donkey   Australia

Opens on a young tramp in the woods. As song starts up – "The Big Rock Candy Mountains" – he sees a new pair of boots (certainly needed) hanging from a tree. The tale and his travels continue and so does his luck as he finds increasingly smart forms of transportation… a donkey…a cart for the donkey… a tractor in a field… an old jalopy in a barn. And when that conks out, he's only walked 200 yards before he's looking at a shiny, new silver Prius. The new petrol-electric Toyota Prius. Keep Moving Forward.

Saatchi & Saatchi, Sydney
CD: David Nobay
CW: Scott McBurnie / David Nobay
AD: David Nobay / Scott McBurnie
AP: Scott McBurnie

Revolver Films, Sydney
Dir: Steve Rogers
Prod: Michael Ritchie

40 **MINI COOPER** • Counterfeit   USA

The commercial is for an important DVD from the Counter Counterfeit Commission, which warns the public about Mini Coopers. "Get a crash course on how to spot a fake. Hear from humiliated victims". The film takes us overseas to show how in unscrupulous sweatshops they duplicate Mini's signature look. And how people are fooled until (as disaster shots exemplify) they try to park… drive… turn. Send a self-addressed stamped envelope today. www.counterfeitmini.org.

Crispin Porter + Bogusky, Miami
CD: Alex Bogusky / Andrew Keller / Steve O'Connell
CW: Franklin Tipton / Rob Reilly
AD: Paul Stechschulte / Tiffany Kosel

**Hungry Man (Santa Monica) /
Jodaf Mixer (Sao Paulo)**
Dir: Bryan Buckley
Prod: Steve Orent / Ralph Laucella

41 VOLKSWAGEN GOLF GTI • For Boys Who Were Always Men | 31st | Germany

Cut to rock track "Devil in me", vignettes from the seventies show little toddlers acting like they already were men. One gets off his potty to pee standing up. One, playing football in the yard, viciously fouls his Dad. Other's swivel round in street to leer at mini-skirted legs … pick out Hot Cars magazine at the news stall … scratch their bums in public just like big guys do … even display manly elbow postures in their prams. The new Golf GTI – "For boys who were always men".

DDB Germany, Berlin
CD: Amir Kassaei / Wofgang Schneider / Mathias Stiller
CW: Ulrich Luetzenkirchen
AD: Sandra Schilling
AP: Marion Lange

@radical.media, Berlin
Dir: Steve Miller
Prod: Christiane Lochte / Ben Schneider

42 TOYOTA VIOS • Bait | Malaysia

Opens on a jogger on a track in glorious country – it could even be the banks of Loch Ness. He stops to admire a beautiful car parked at the water's edge. As he reaches to touch it, the car falls over, revealed to be a cardboard cutout. With which a monster erupts from the lake and a giant tentacle snatches the jogger and pulls him in. Title: "The Irresistible Vios". Tentacle re-emerges to re-adjust the cutout. Title: "You'll want one".

Saatchi & Saatchi, Petaling Jaya
CD: Henry Yap / Edmund Choe
CW: Primus Nair
AD: Ong Kien Hoe
AP: Shirren Lim

Passion Pictures Malaysia, Kuala Lumpur
Dir: Jamie Quah
Prod: Karen D'Silva / Razlan Ramdan / Affendi Harjoh

43 RENAULT CLIO • Scarecrow 28th Argentina

A red Clio is driving through rolling countryside. The driver is … a scarecrow. Song. "This will be my time to go away". Clio takes track down to a deserted beach. Scarecrow spends a lovely afternoon there as gulls swoop and waves lap around his wooden stumps. Sun is setting as Clio takes road again. Back to a field where a guy, the car's owner, has been standing in to give the scarecrow a break. They hug, then scarecrow returns to work. Renault Clio. Big Inside. (Like a Clio owner, it would seem).

Lowe A&B, Buenos Aires
CD: Maximiliano Anselmo
CW: Pablo Minces
AP: José Bustos

Pioneer, Buenos Aires
Dir: Luciano Podcaminsky
Prod: Flora Fernandez Marengo

44 RENAULT ESPACE • Hector France

In a busy station, we see a tiny, 2D paper cartoon character – Hector – slip through the crack in the waiting room door and dodge the tramping shoes of the commuters to hitch a ride on freight train. Song up: "Going Up The Country" by Canned Heat. Once in open countryside he alights, explores forests and fields and ends up contemplating a majestic view from the top of a mountain. Back in the waiting room we see the comic strip in a newspaper, whence Hector has escaped. "Isn't space the ultimate luxury?" Renault Espace.

Publicis Conseil, Paris
CD: Hervé Plumet / Olivier Altmann
CW: Thierry Lebec
AD: Bénédicte Potel
AP: Muriel Allegrini

Bandits, Suresnes / WAM, Boulogne-Billancourt
Dir: Dom / Nic
Prod: Philippe Dupuis-Mendel

45 MERCEDES-BENZ CABRIOLET • The Sounds of Summer | 15th | Germany

A sound wave print across the screen morphs into virtual 3D landscapes. Throaty car engine purrs into life. The equaliser graphic transforms into a succession of synthetic images: open road with trees … horse riders passing … a train chugging through the countryside … mountains and pine forests … a windswept ocean shore. While birdsong, buzz of bees, horses hooves thudding, shriek of gulls, children's laughter help paint the pictures for us. Hear the summer. In a Mercedes-Benz convertible.

Springer & Jacoby, Hamburg
CD: Till Hohmann / Alex Thomsen
CW: Fiorian Kähler / Fiorian Pagel
AD: Justus v. Engelhardt / Tobias Gradert-Hinzpeter

Sehsucht, Hamburg
Dir: Ole Peters / Timo Schädel
Prod: Andreas Coutsoumbelis

46 HONDA DIESEL • Grrr | 1st | Great Britain

Can hate be a good thing? A tranquil animated world of rainbows, lily ponds and green meadows is invaded by a fleet of spluttering, smoking, dirty old diesel engines. The little creatures who inhabit this technicolour paradise, get angry and using their hate for the better, destroy the offending engines one by one. Finally they herald the entry of a shiny new incarnation, the environment-friendly Honda Diesel, which cruises gently over the joyous landscape, making no more than a delicate fluttering sound. Honda. The Power of Dreams.

Wieden+Kennedy, London
CD: Tony Davidson / Kim Papworth
CW: Sean Thompson / Michael Russoff /
Richard Russell
AD: Sean Thompson / Michael Russoff /
Richard Russell
AP: Charlie Tinson / Rob Steiner

Nexus Productions, London
Dir: Adam Foulkes / Alan Smith
Prod: Julie Parfitt / Chris O'Reilly

In a big city, people crowding sidewalks and crossing streets are as normal. But all the cars on the roads are superbly crafted, life-size toys. A blue roadster with a wind-up key, a pink convertible in bakelite, a cop car with paper cops pasted on windscreen, a yellow Lego toytown mini-bus and giant Matchbox replicas. Till, with music up, a real-life, head-turning Peugeot 407 appears on a bridge, weaving through the toys. Super: "Playtime is over." Peugeot 407.

BETC Euro RSCG, Paris
CD: Rémi Babinet
CW: Rémi Noel
AD: Eric Holden
AP: David Green

Wanda Productions, La Plaine Saint-Denis
Dir: Philippe André

It's late at night as little white car drives into a petrol station. The pump attendant sees the young driver yawning and looking mighty sleepy. As he fills the car, the garage guy starts to whistle a well-known lullaby and he gently rocks the vehicle to send the driver peacefully to sleep. He then pushes the little car over next to a line of others, which also have sleeping drivers. Total. You won't come to us by chance.

CLM BBDO, Issy les Moulineaux

CD: Pascal Gregoire / Anne de Maupeou
CW: Jean-Francois Sacco
AD: Gilles Fichteberg
AP: Pierre Marcus / France Monnet

Quad Productions, Paris

Dir: Remy Belvaux
Prod: Nicolas Duval

49   VIRGIN ATLANTIC UPPER CLASS • Love Story   42nd   South Africa

A singer in a gay club sings his song – "How Deep is Your Love?", the Bee Gees – for one customer only. Idyllic cutaways show the two guys boating on a lake, cavorting on a beach, canoodling in a photo booth, getting hot and steamy at a pottery wheel, sharing a foaming bath and finally at the altar. Cut to reality and an airplane with the fat guy snoring on the other's shoulder. "If you wanted to sleep with him, you would have married him". Virgin Atlantic Upper Class. Get your own flat bed suite.

Net#work BBDO, Johannesburg
CD: Mike Schalit
CW: John Davenport
AD: Philip Ireland
AP: Caroline Switala

Velocity Films, Johannesburg
Dir: Greg Gray
Prod: Helena Woodfine

50   GOL AIRLINES • Cages   Brazil

Gol are the first cut price airline in Brazil (the Easyjet of South America). A sweet latin dance tune plays under, as camera shows a succession of open windows which have open cages painted on the brickwork around them. We see such windows in a top flat in a stucco house, a chalet with flower boxes, an apartment with washing on the balcony, a bungalow with blue shutters, and many more. "Now everyone can fly". Buenos Aires to Sao Paulo for just $100. Gol. Smart Airline.

AlmapBBDO, Sao Paulo
CD: Cassio Zanatta / Giba Lages
CW: Dulcidio Caldeira
AD: Cesar Finamori
AP: Egisto Betti

Republika Filmes, Sao Paulo
Dir: Carlos Manga Junior

We meet a family who have inherited (from their Uncle Jasper) exceptionally large noses that make loud, whistling noises when they breathe. Their whistling schnozzes get them into embarrassing situations – like in box at the theatre, or in a field with a fierce black dog, or in the library, or in village store where maiden misinterprets the innocent man's whistle. But when they come together for vacation at Holiday Inn (we see them at the pool at night) their combined noise makes lovely music. Relax it's Holiday Inn.

Fallon, Minneapolis
CD: Bruce Bildsten
CW: Reuben Hower
AD: Todd Riddle
AP: Kate Talbott

Biscuit Filmworks, Los Angeles / Stillking, Prague
Dir: Noam Murro
Prod: Shawn Lacy Tessaro / Zuzana de Pagter

52a SONY PLAYSTATION 2 • Athletes   12th   Great Britain

Title over: "Life on the Playstation". In African grasslands, scores of young track athletes limber up. VO: "Summer, and de athletes are gathering. The males show off, competing for the females attention." But men holding dummies are hiding in the long grass. VO: "The ventriloquists are planning a challenge". A young ventriloquist charges prematurely. The older ventriloquists throw their voices thus confusing the athletes causing them to run straight towards them. A limping athlete is picked off. "Fun, anyone?" Playstation 2.

TBWA\London
CD: Trevor Beattie
CW: Paul Silburn / Tony McTear
AD: Paul Silburn / Tony McTear
AP: Diane Croll

Large, London
Dir: Daniel Kleinman
Prod: Johnnie Frankel

52b SONY PLAYSTATION 2 • Golfers   12th   Great Britain

Title over: "Life on the Playstation". As if in a wildebeest migration in a wildlife documentary, a huge herd of golfers files towards an African river. VO: "Life on de Playstation can spell great danger for de golfers". A tribe of porn stars is basking erotically on the river bank. The golfers start to cross, the porn stars pounce. We see that "a lone golfer is no match for three fit females". Meanwhile a large male takes a golfer from behind. On the opposite bank, the survivors congratulate each other. "Fun, anyone?" Playstation 2.

TBWA\London
CD: Trevor Beattie
CW: Paul Silburn / Tony McTear
AD: Paul Silburn / Tony McTear
AP: Diane Croll

Large, London
Dir: Daniel Kleinman
Prod: Johnnie Frankel

52c SONY PLAYSTATION 2 • Porn Stars   12th   Great Britain

Title over: "Life on the Playstation". A small group of porn stars laze around beside a water hole in Africa. The women in their Anne Summers undies take to the water and playfully splash each other. VO: "These females are restless. They start to play with each other, and soon get excited". On the bank, two hunky male porn stars – one black, one white – leer appreciatively (they obviously enjoy their work). The studs are joined by a passing football mascot. "Fun, anyone?" Playstation 2.

TBWA\London
CD: Trevor Beattie
CW: Paul Silburn / Tony McTear
AD: Paul Silburn / Tony McTear
AP: Diane Croll

Large, London
Dir: Daniel Kleinman
Prod: Johnnie Frankel

53 AJINOMOTO STADIUM • Husky Girls   21st   Japan

A young dude arrives in town and is excited by the beauty of the girls. The only setback – as he discovers in the college lecture hall... the canteen... with a school choir he passes... in street encounters – all the lovely girls have gravely, husky voices! Till he (literally) bumps into a plain young Miss, whose voice is normal. They end up in bed. He chose her for her voice, he says. "I don't go to the games", she explains. Cut to stadium: gorgeous females shouting themselves hoarse. "Shout all you like". Ajinimoto Stadium.

Dentsu, Tokyo
CD: Yuya Furukawa
CW: Hiroyo Kanehako
AD: Hiroyo Kanehako

Dentsu Tec, Tokyo
Dir: Jun Kawanishi
Prod: Maho Tada / Hidetoshi Nakano

54 CLUB ATLETICO DE MADRID • Member #1 — Spain

Camera roams around a cosy flat, as we hear an old man's voice, "At 63, I quit smoking. When I was 70, I gave up drinking anisette…" Camera shows objects that relate to his narrative – ashtray, bottle and glass etc. He's also succeeded in giving up wine at mealtimes… salt… coffee… betting… playing cards. End on old boy himself watching football on TV, "But that blasted Atletico! It kills me. It keeps me alive". We've been visiting the home of Senor Agustin de la Fuente Quintana, "Member #1 of Atletico de Madrid Club".

SRA Rushmore, Madrid
CD: Miguel Garcia Vizcaino
AD: Marta Rico
AP: Jorge Martinez

Lee Films, Madrid
Dir: Nicolas Caicoya
Prod: Pato Castellanos

55a BC LIONS • Vending Machine — 36th — Canada

Opens on a woman putting money in a vending machine. The candy bar gets stuck. She gives machine a half-hearted shove and starts to leave. A man who's seen this challenges her, "What! You're not gonna just walk away and give up? That's yours! Nobody else's! Go in and get it!" The woman thumps, beats, karate kicks and even shoulder charges the vending machine, as man's cheers intensify. The bar drops. Man punches air – "Yes!" Title: "Cheering Works". BC Lions logo.

Rethink, Vancouver
CD: Ian Grais / Chris Staples
CW: Andy Linardatos
AD: Ian Grais
AP: Christine Pacheco

Spy Films, Toronto
Dir: Trevor Cornish
Prod: Bonnie Chung

55b **BC LIONS** • Cashier 36th Canada

Opens at a check out in a supermarket. A woman cashier is doing things very slowly. A young colleague in an apron sees this. "Hey, Gail. Let's get things going here, Gail", he exhorts her. "Pick up the pace a little!" Gail starts to hustle. Shoppers join in with encouragement and support. Gail is soon going great guns. They all whoop and leap around as she triumphantly completes the order. Title: "Cheering Works". BC Lions logo.

Rethink, Vancouver
CD: Ian Grais / Chris Staples
CW: Andy Linardatos
AD: Ian Grais
AP: Christine Pacheco

Spy Films, Toronto
Dir: Trevor Cornish
Prod: Bonnie Chung

56 **LEO'S SPORTS CLUB** • Nuts Germany

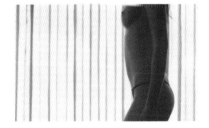  

Opens in a pleasant apartment. We hear the sound of a shower being switched off. A highly attractive young woman pads in naked and past the bed, drying herself with a big white towel. She crosses to the table where there's a bowl of walnuts. She takes a nut and cracks it between the cheeks of her bottom. She glances round at camera, as she eats the nut. Pan down to her Leo's Sports Club bag on the floor. www.leos.sportsclub.de

Xynias Wetzel Werbeagentur, Munich

CD: Marc Strotmann / Chris Mayrhofer
CW: Daniel Schaefer
AD: Volker Schmidt
AP: Corinna Bornemann

Neue Sentimental Film, Berlin
Dir: Lars Knorn
Prod: Stephan Braungardt

57 HUNGARIAN DANCE ACADEMY• Ballet Needs Boys   Hungary

The Dance Academy in Budapest is desperately short of male applicants. In the signature scene from Swan Lake, the lovely young ballerina totters on her toes in perfect pirouettes clutching her hands in front of her. She seems to be wringing them in anguish. The other ballerinas flutter gracefully as the leading lady lays down towards camera in her dying routine. She sets down the object she was holding – a pickle jar she couldn't open. "Ballet Needs Boys". The Hungarian Dance Academy.

Leo Burnett Budapest
CD: Milos Ilic
CW: Leonardo Pinto / Taricicio Nunes / Agnes Fazakas
AD: Milos Ilic
AP: Ildiko Orosz / Ilona Baroti

Filmpartners, Budapest
Dir: Milos Ilic / Imre Juhasz
Prod: Ildiko Orosz / Ilona Baroti

58 TOHO CINEMAS • Leaving Office   Japan

An office worker sticks a pen up her nose. "I'm leaving early, I've got a nose bleed". The supervisor says to cut it out. Banging her head on wastebasket to get a headache doesn't work either. So she crosses to her boss and rubs his hand around her breasts. "Sexual harassment! I'm going home". She then spills coffee on him and forcibly removes his shirt and trousers. Ends on girl sprinting down street pursued by boss in Y-fronts, shoes and socks. Title over: "Movies are calling me". Ends on happy girl in theatre. Toho Cinemas.

Build Creativehaus, Tokyo
CD: Keita Yamada
CW: Keita Yamada

Dentsu Tec, Tokyo
Dir: Akira Nagai
Prod: Kimio Miyata

59a CANADIAN SHORT FILM FESTIVAL • Establishing a Character   3rd   Canada

The teacher of a 'Short Film Actors Workshop' interrupts two students rehearsing a scene from classical theatre. "Sit down. I don't get it. Who is who?" Establishing a character in a short film has gotta be quick, he explains. "Go again Favius", he commands. Favius starts up, he grabs Favius' nipple and twists. "Good guy, bad guy, 2 seconds." Students gape in awe of their teacher's genius.

Taxi, Toronto
CD: Zak Mroueh
CW: Pete Breton
AD: Dave Douglass
AP: Sam Benson

Untitled, Toronto
Dir: Tim Godsall

59b CANADIAN SHORT FILM FESTIVAL • Special F/X   3rd   Canada

The teacher of a 'Short Film Actors Workshop' dismisses traditional special F/X as expensive and time-consuming. He affixes a smoking cigarette in a bulldog clip to his trouser flies. "And look.. I'm Brigadoon walking the Scottish moors.. or gorillas in the mist. You're all wrong. It's me. Ian Hediger. I'm acting. Magic." The students are all agog and wonderstruck at their teacher's craft and wizardry.

Taxi, Toronto
CD: Zak Mroueh
CW: Pete Breton
AD: Dave Douglass
AP: Sam Benson

Untitled, Toronto
Dir: Tim Godsall
Prod: James Davis

59c CANADIAN SHORT FILM FESTIVAL • Good Cop/Bad Cop 3rd Canada

Two 'Short Film Actors Workshop' students play the cops in an interrogation scene. One bullies the suspect, the other is nice to her, the dialogue is lengthy. Teacher interrupts. Good cop/bad cop is hard to do in a short film, he concedes. Luckily he's developed a method – the Hediger method. He faces the suspect; "Confess, bitch. Nice hair." Canadian Film Centre - Short Film Festival.

Taxi, Toronto
CD: Zak Mroueh
CW: Pete Breton
AD: Dave Douglass
AP: Sam Benson

Untitled, Toronto
Dir: Tim Godsall
Prod: James Davis

59d CANADIAN SHORT FILM FESTIVAL • Craft Awards 3rd Canada

A male and a female compere are at twin podiums on a stage. A beefy, bouncer-type stands between them. We're at the Short Film Craft Awards ceremony and the proceedings are befittingly brisk. The MC rattles off the categories and winners' names without drawing breath: the bouncer throws the statuettes out into the room to crashland on the recipients' tables. "Oh, toss him another for Best Sound Editing". In no time at all the MC is thanking the audience – "Without you there'd be no short film".

Taxi, Toronto
CD: Zak Mroueh
CW: Pete Breton
AD: Dave Douglass
AP: Sam Benson

Untitled, Toronto
Dir: Tim Godsall
Prod: James Davis

60a **L'EQUIPE SPORTS NEWSPAPER** • Mother ⟨32nd⟩ France

A man, carrying folded newspaper, takes seat on sofa at home and picks up TV remote. His wife enters with a cup of coffee, which she drops and screams and screams. The man is momentarily puzzled, then picks up his L'Equipe and buries himself in it's pages. Wife stops screaming. "Ah, c'est toi, cheri". Everday. Every Sport. L'Equipe. "Tu veux un camomille?" we hear wife ask.

DDB Paris
CD: Alexandre Hervé / Sylvain Thirache
CW: Céline Landa
AD: Benjamin Marchal
AP: Agathe Michaux

Soixan7e Quin5e, Paris
Dir: Jonathan Herman
Prod: Greg Panteix

60b **L'EQUIPE SPORTS NEWSPAPER** • Child ⟨32nd⟩ France

A man, carrying a folded newspaper, enters his little son's room at night to tuck him in. He sits down on bed. Boy sits up in fright and starts to scream and scream – "Maman!" Dad is startled then understands and grabs his newspaper, L'Equipe, and buries himself in its pages. Boy relaxes – "Ah, c'est toi, Papa". He enfolds his dad and the newspaper in a big hug. Every day. Every sport. L'Equipe.

DDB Paris
CD: Alexandre Hervé / Sylvain Thirache
CW: Céline Landa
AD: Benjamin Marchal
AP: Agathe Michaux

Soixan7e Quin5e, Paris
Dir: Jonathan Herman
Prod: Greg Panteix

61 **SCIENCE WORLD** • Boardroom `25th` Canada

Opens in a boardroom before a meeting. The visiting team enters and is greeted: "Ted! You remember Annette?" Ted and Annette partake in a lingering kiss. Annette then turns to second man, "You must be Jeffrey", and gives him same treatment, while Linda from accounting has a good old snog with Ted. The ladies then kiss deeply. And so, after "Ted, you old dog, how's that golf game?", do the guys. Super: "Shaking hands spreads more germs than kissing". Science World. We can explain.

Rethink, Vancouver

CD:	Ian Grais / Chris Staples
CW:	Rob Tarry
AD:	Rob Sweetman
AP:	Jacqueline Burgmann

Radke Films, Toronto

Dir:	Michael Downing

62 **MTV** • Wedding Romania

The local pop group bangs out a tune, as guests at a wedding bop away. The keyboard player surveys the room morosely. A dude in Errol Flynn moustache and leather coat is dancing suggestively with the bride. The groom, who doesn't like this, lurches to his feet with a bottle. The keyboard player hastily assembles a frame and holds it over the scene, as groom smashes bottle over rival's head, grabs for his bride, and falls on his face. Frame features MTV logo in corner and caption "Made in Romania".

McCann Erickson Romania, Bucharest

CD:	Adrian Botan
CW:	Emilian Arsenoaiei
AD:	Radu Tinc
AP:	Octavian Stavila

Castel Films, Bucharest

Dir:	Radu Muntean
Prod:	Octavian Stavila

63   DIRECTV • Fathers & Sons   Argentina

Opens on a DirecTV satellite dish. Song up and under, "Mr Sandman". Camera shows a succession of fathers and sons watching TV together. It's uncanny to see how not just their physical features but also their reactions to what they are watching, are so identical.

The last vignette, however, shows a big black son and a tiny white dad. Then son crosses his hands on his chest in exactly his dad's gesture. Dad looks pleased and pats son on the knee. "Give him DirecTV for Father's Day."

Lowe A&B, Buenos Aires
CD: Maximiliano Anselmo
CW: Pablo Minces
AD: Maximiliano Anselmo
AP: José Bustos

Bendercine, Buenos Aires
Dir: Claudio Prestia
Prod: Paula Mazzei / Jacqueline Lijtensten

64a   RADIO DONNA • Gay   Belgium

In a cosy sitting room a young man seems to be thinking something over. His parents read their newspapers. Suddenly he prances to his feet, rips off his shirt and sings a song ("The smell of leather brings me in the mood/ tight pants – wow! – they feel so good") to tell Mum and Dad he's gay. A pair of aggressively homo-erotic specimens flank him as backing singers. Far from being dismayed, parents enjoy the song and nod along and tap feet to the beat. Thank you for the Music. Radio Donna.

LG&F, Brussels
CD: Christophe Ghewy / Paul Wauters
CW: T Driesen / J van den Broeckl /
       I Vandevyver / T Jacobs
AD: T Jacobs / I Vandevyver /
       J van den Broeck / T Driesen
AP: Myriam Maes

Czar.be, Brussels / Bonkers, Brussels
Dir: Matthijs Van Heijningen
Prod: Ruben Goots / Saskia Verboven

64b RADIO DONNA • Marriage   Belgium

A fat bloke is shovelling down his food at a roadside diner, his pregnant partner watches him glumly. Suddenly she's on her feet singing him and all assembled a catchy Kylie Minogue number with new lyrics saying she's dumping him for his boss. "And he love mo-dern art/ And his friends don't fart" being sample lyrics. Music makes even the worst news a pleasure to the ears, because boyfriend seems to like her song, nodding away as she leaves. Thank you for the Music. Radio Donna.

LG&F, Brussels
CD: Christophe Ghewy / Paul Wauters
CW: T Driesen / J van den Broeckl /
        I Vandevyver / T Jacobs
AD: T Jacobs / I Vandevyver /
        J van den Broeck / T Driesen
AP: Myriam Maes

Czar.be, Brussels / Bonkers, Brussels
Dir: Matthijs Van Heijningen
Prod: Ruben Goots / Saskia Verboven

65a VH1 TV CHANNEL • Parents' Day   11th   USA

It's parents' day in a classroom at an elementary school. One father, looking like the lead singer of an 80's glamrock band, interrupts the teacher, who is explaining the syllabus – "Hi, everybody, I'm Jenny's father". Cue for guitar chord, pyrotechnics and smoke. Same stage effects happen each time he speaks, but he's reassured by teacher's answers – "I always wanted Jenny to grow up in a normal environment". "A musician's life is more than just videos". VH1. Beyond music.

La Comunidad, Miami Beach
CD: Joaquin Mollá / José Mollá / Ricardo Vior
CW: Martin Ialfen / Leo Pial
AD: Ricardo Vior / Julian Montessano
AP: Facundo Perez

Landia Republica, Buenos Aires
Dir: Andy Fogwill / Agustin Alberdi
Prod: Claudio Amoedo

A rap artist is at an outdoor market buying apples. Each time we cut, from stall holder to rapper, music cuts in and several dancers' bottoms, shaking to the beat in glitzy thongs, are to be seen right behind his head. The rapper chooses his fruit carefully and even haggles a bit about the price. The stall holder accommodates him. The bottoms keep shaking. "A musician's life is more than just videos". VH1. Beyond music.

La Comunidad, Miami Beach
CD: Joaquin Mollá / José Mollá / Ricardo Vior
CW: Martin Jalfen / Leo Prat
AD: Ricardo Vior / Julian Montessano
AP: Facundo Perez

Landia Republica, Buenos Aires
Dir: Andy Fogwill / Agustin Alberdi
Prod: Claudio Amoedo

66a **RCA DLP TV** • Squished Locker Room   USA

A TV commentator interviews soccer players in a locker room. All seem to be pressed up against a giant sheet of glass. Cut to the field of play for more squished faces – players in a "wall" facing a free kick, the ref with the ball, a blatant foul, ref giving red card. Everything from the locker room interviews to the action on the pitch is squashed, as though playing within the six inch space behind your TV screen. The world's thinnest flat screen TV. The HD Scenium Profile Series. RCA.

Publicis, New York
CD: Mike Long
CW: Brian Platt / Josh Greenspan
AD: Mike Long
AP: Nadia Blake

Czar.us, New York
Dir: Lionel Goldstein
Prod: Steven Shore

66b **RCA DLP TV** • Squished Concert   USA

We see a typical rock concert from a different perspective. The group on stage, as they cavort and posture, seem like they are squashed up against a giant sheet of glass. Even the lead singer's shades are pushed off his face. The groupies in the crowd are similarly squished, as if into six inches of space, as they sway and gesticulate. Pull back shows these pictures are on a big TV. The world's thinnest flat screen TV. The HD Scenium Profile Series. RCA.

Publicis, New York
CD: Mike Long
CW: Brian Platt / Josh Greenspan
AD: Mike Long
AP: Nadia Blake

Czar.us, New York
Dir: Lionel Goldstein
Prod: Steven Shore

67 HEWLETT PACKARD • Picture Book — USA

Jaunty song "Picture Book" under, as a group of citizens pose in a square in Stockholm. Each carries an open white picture frame, which they raise to frame their heads as camera clicks. And which becomes a constant graphic linking further scenes in streets and city parks, by the sea shore, trampolining, and also at a fancy dress ball. Everyone plays with pictures and plays with reality in this homage to the ease, fun and magic of photo-making. HP Digital Photography. Click. Print. Invent. You and HP.

Goodby Silverstein & Partners, San Francisco
CD: Rich Silverstein / Steve Simpson / John Norman
CW: Steve Simpson
AD: John Norman
AP: Josh Reynolds / Brian Coate

Tool of North America, Santa Monica / Paranoid Projects @ Tool, Santa Monica
Dir: Francois Vogel
Prod: Claude Letessier / Jennifer Siege

68a OLYMPUS DIGITAL CAMERA • Red-Eyed Baby — The Netherlands

  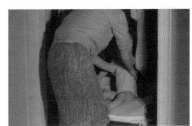

A man arrives home after work – "I'm home, I'm here". As if drawn, he goes down hallway to the bedroom. Sitting on the floor is a very pretty baby – whose eyes are red. Man retreats to kitchen, confronts his wife: "I told you that freaks me out!" Wife sighs, gives him a look, then goes and puts the baby in the closet. "Would you save or delete a red-eyed baby?" Olympus Digital. What you choose to remember.

Springer & Jacoby, Amsterdam
CD: Aris Theophilakis / Murray White
CW: Murray White / Sharon Cleary
AD: Chris Pugmire
AP: Ronald Milton

Tony Petersen Film, Hamburg / Biscuit Filmworks, Los Angeles
Dir: Noam Murro
Prod: Mandy Kothe

68b OLYMPUS DIGITAL CAMERA • Distorted Dogs   The Netherlands

A woman having coffee at her friend's place looks suddenly alarmed. "What is that?" Entering the kitchen – a dog with an enormous, distorted head. Two more of the gruesome creatures appear in another doorway. Lady of the house maintains they're beautiful, telling her friend, "It really is going to be all right". "Would you save or delete distorted dogs?" Olympus Digital. What you choose to remember.

Springer & Jacoby, Amsterdam
CD: Aris Theophilakis / Murray White
CW: Murray White / Sharon Cleary
AD: Chris Pugmire
AP: Ronald Milton

Tony Petersen Film, Hamburg / Biscuit Filmworks, Los Angeles
Dir: Noam Murro
Prod: Mandy Kothe

68c OLYMPUS DIGITAL CAMERA • Cropped Tourists   The Netherlands

A man answers insistent knocking on his apartment door. Outside are an older American couple with the tops of their heads missing. Angry woman: "You promised to mail us with that photo from the Eiffel Tower". The man pleads with them to go away, go home. Woman: "Gimme that photo". Man retreats and hides under his duvet. "Would you delete or email cropped tourists?" Olympus Digital. What you choose to remember.

Springer & Jacoby, Amsterdam
CD: Aris Theophilakis / Murray White
CW: Murray White / Sharon Cleary
AD: Chris Pugmire
AP: Ronald Milton

Tony Petersen Film, Hamburg / Biscuit Filmworks, Los Angeles
Dir: Noam Murro
Prod: Mandy Kothe

69   UNEFON MOBILE PHONE • Leg   35th   Mexico

A distraught woman on the cell phone to her boyfriend, "That is a leg, Juan Carlos". He replies gently, "No, honey, where do you see the leg?" "There's a woman's leg behind your head". Juan Carlos' sweet talking skills know no bounds. "The wedding, it's got you nervous… besides I love you". They say goodnight and girl gazes at the photo on her phone, which we now see for first time. (And there definitely is a leg). She kisses his image on the phone. "Photos. What is new as always". Unefon.

S2 Mexico, Mexico City
CD: Eduardo Perez / Santiago Chaumont / Alvaro Zunini
CW: Eduardo Perez / Santiago Chaumont / Alvaro Zunini
AD: Santiago Chaumont / Alvaro Zunini
AP: Valeria Chavez

Garcia Bross y Asociados, Mexico City
Dir: Simon Bross
Prod: Beto Bross

70   SAGEM MYX5-2 MOBILE PHONE • Tokyo   43rd   France

A young man is taking photos of random objects on his mobile – a lavatory, a taxicab sign, soda pop, a washing machine in a laundrette, a hotel sign, a burger and fries, a fork, rotisserie chicken, a comb, condoms, et al. Next he's on a plane, then at Narita airport, then in downtown Tokyo. Approaching a gaggle of Japanese schoolgirls, he flashes the photo of the toilet bowl on his mobile. It works – they point him to the nearest washroom. Sagem. Simply Smart.

Publicis Conseil, Paris
CD: Olivier Altmann
CW: Guilhem Arnal
AD: Robin de Lestrade
AP: Nicolas Buisset

Soixan7e Qui5e, Paris
Dir: Johan Renck
Prod: Emmanuel Guiraud

71 CENTRAAL BEHEER INSURANCE • Lion · The Netherlands

We join a family in their car at a safari park. There's Dad, Mum, 2 kids and Oma. A gaggle of lions come to investigate the car – one even gets paws up on hood. Dad honks, lions retreat. As they drive home after a fun day out, boy starts up "Wimaway" song, which they all join in – "The Lion Sleeps Tonight". A cutaway shows a very big lion is riding on the roof of their car. It ducks deftly as car enters garage. "Just Call Us". Centraal Beheer – the insurance company from Apeldoorn.

DDB Amsterdam
CD: Sikko Gerkema
CW: Sikko Gerkema
AD: Sanne Braam
AP: Chantal Gulpers

Czar.nl, Amsterdam
Dir: Steve Ayson
Prod: Sybrig Stork

72a HSBC • Hole in One · Great Britain

A foursome – three Japanese gents and their American guest - on a golf course with Mount Fuji in the background. The American hits a sweet three iron from the tee. Ball soars over valley to heart of green, trickles into hole. VO: "In America, if you hit a hole in one, you're expected to buy everyone a drink. However, in Japan, it's traditional to buy your playing partners expensive gifts." Mix to next day, same hole. The Japanese admire each other's Rolexes. The American pulls his shot on purpose. But it rebounds from a tree onto the green and down the hole. HSBC. The world's local bank.

Lowe, London
CD: Damon Collins
CW: Sam Cartmell / Jason Lawes
AD: Jason Lawes / Sam Cartmell
AP: Russell Benson

Partizan, London
Dir: Eric Lynne

72b HSBC • Okey Doke — Great Britain

Shades of "Motorcycle Diaries" (and similar great cinematography) as we join a guy who's travelling across South America by motorbike. Music is Jimmy Hendrix's "Easy Rider". In every country he is greeted by friendly locals giving the OK sign (a circle made by thumb and index finger), a gesture he soon adopts. This is his undoing, however, when he makes it to a burly diner owner in Brazil (where it means "up yours" – a very rude version of). "We never underestimate the importance of local knowledge." HSBC. The world's local bank.

Lowe, London
CD: Damon Collins
CW: Vince Squibb
AD: Vince Squibb
AP: Chales Crisp

Gorgeous Enterprises, London
Dir: Chris Palmer
Prod: Rupert Smythe

73 AXION YOUTH BANKING • Braille — Belgium

We're at a sort of gaudy shrine. The attraction is a teenage Scottish boy, the spots on whose face spell out beautiful stories in Braille. Various pilgrims bear witness to their personal experiences. If he eats Chinese food, the Braille comes out in Chinese. His canny family does a busy trade in pictures, souvenir plates, candles. Ends on boy at home with indoor pool and luxury bed chamber. "The day you have money you will need a bank". Axion. Banking for young people.

Duval Guillaume Brussels
CD: Jens Mortier
CW: Katrien Bottez
AD: Peter Ampe
AP: Andreas Hasle

Czar.be, Brussels
Dir: Lionel Goldstein
Prod: Ruben Goots

74   THAI LIFE INSURANCE • Everlasting Love   Thailand

Beautiful images show a very old man, who gets up early, makes soup, and sets off on a 20 kilometre trek through lovely countryside, with the soup and his 2-string fiddle. We end at a grave up a mountain where the man has placed the soup and is playing a haunting tune. Grandpa Huw has done this every morning for nearly 30 years. When he married he promised his wife that he would make soup for her and play her favourite song for her every day until the day that he dies. How much do you care for your loved ones? Thai Life Insurance.

Ogilvy & Mather Thailand, Bangkok
CD: Korn Tepintarapiraksa
CW: Korn Tepintarapiraksa / Kulvadee Doksroy /
       Kris Spindler
AD: Korn Tepintarapiraksa
AP: Yuthapong Varanukrokchoke

Phenomena, Bangkok
Dir: Thanonchai Sornsrivichai
Prod: Piyawan Mungkang

75a   AMERIQUEST MORTGAGE • Mini Mart   33rd   USA

A guy walks into Bob's market on cell phone to his wife. He's saying she's paying too much for a deck. "You're being robbed!" Shopkeeper behind counter hears this and on his CCTV sees the guy reaching in his jacket. He sprays the man with Mace, then whacks him with a baseball bag and his wife finishes him off with an electric cattle prod. Titles: "Don't judge too quickly". "We won't". Ameriquest. An open-minded, equal-opportunity lender.

DDB Los Angeles, Venice, CA
CD: Mark Monteiro
CW: Pat McKay / Josh Fell
AD.   Feh Tarty / Michael Mittelstaedt
AP: Vanessa Macadam

MJZ, Los Angeles
Dir: Craig Gillespie

75b AMERIQUEST MORTGAGE • Parking Meter — 33rd — USA

A guy at a parking meter drops his coin which rolls down a drain. He sees warden just down the road giving tickets. He goes into the nearest shop for change and bumps into his sister-in-law plus her little daughter on the way out. The guy from the shop – a porn shop – follows: "Forget your wallet". Sister-in-law sees him in a new light. Titles: "Don't judge too quickly". "We won't". Ameriquest. An open-minded, equal-opportunity lender.

DDB Los Angeles, Venice, CA
CD: Mark Monteiro
CW: Pat McKay / Josh Fell
AD: Feh Tarty / Michael Mittelstaedt
AP: Vanessa Macadam

MJZ, Los Angeles
Dir: Craig Gillespie

75c AMERIQUEST MORTGAGE • Mother-in-Law — 33rd — USA

A man and his wife, in the kitchen in the morning, are having a recurring quarrel. "I don't hate your mother", she snarls and heads upstairs with said elderly relative's breakfast tray. A pillow has fallen from bed, wife picks it up to put it back. Husband, who has followed with maple syrup jug, mistakes the scene for an attempt on his sleeping mother's life. Carpet gets all maple-y. Titles: "Don't judge too quickly". "We won't". Ameriquest. An open-minded, equal-opportunity lender.

DDB Los Angeles, Venice, CA
CD: Mark Monteiro
CW: Pat McKay / Josh Fell
AD: Feh Tarty / Michael Mittelstaedt
AP: Vanessa Macadam

MJZ, Los Angeles
Dir: Craig Gillespie

76a **EBAY** • Clocks   USA

We see a man in his home. Every square inch of wall is occupied by clocks. He is polishing one. Man turns to find his living room is packed with people, each holding a different clock for his inspection. His garden outside and the neighbourhood right down to the beach are also thronged with people showing him clocks. The man picks one: the rest of crowd sigh. "There are thousands of people who have what you love. How will you find them?" eBay. The power of all of us.

Goodby Silverstein & Partners, San Francisco

CD: Jeff Goodby / Jamie Barrett / Rob Palmer
CW: Jamie Barrett
AD: Rob Palmer
AP: Cindy Fluitt / Mary Jane Otto

Biscuit Filmworks, Los Angeles

Dir: Noam Murro
Prod: Jay Veal

76b **EBAY** • Toy Boat   USA

A little boy on a beach is called by his parents and forgets his toy boat. Title over: "Cape Cod 1972". The boat is taken by the tide, floats out to sea, rides out storms, is hit by a trawler's propeller, sinks to ocean floor. Years later it is hauled up in some Japanese fishermen's net. Cut to an eBay page advertising the little boat. A man (who would have been a boy of 5 in 1972) gazes at screen in amazed recognition. eBay. The power of all of us.

Goodby Silverstein & Partners, San Francisco

CD: Jeff Goodby / Jamie Barrett / Rob Palmer
CW: Jamie Barrett
AD: Rob Palmer
AP: Cindy Fluitt / Mary Jane Otto

Biscuit Filmworks, Los Angeles

Dir: Noam Murro
Prod: Jay Veal

76c **EBAY** • Belief — USA

A piano tune under, a succession of vignettes depict little acts of human goodness and kindness. A fly poster on a tree "I found your dog" … meals on wheels volunteers … recycling bins … holding elevator doors … pushing car in snow … helping retrieve papers from a spilled briefcase … blood donors … the picking up of litter … a Mum and Dad with two smiling Asian kids (adopted). Etc, Etc. "We began with the belief that people are good". "You proved it". eBay. The power of all of us.

Goodby Silverstein & Partners, San Francisco
CD: Jeff Goodby / Jamie Barrett / Rob Palmer
CW: Jamie Barrett
AD: Rob Palmer
AP: Cindy Fluitt / Mary Jane Otto

Biscuit Filmworks, Los Angeles
Dir: Noam Murro
Prod: Jay Veal

77 **IKEA** • Embla — Sweden

A cheeky little Swedish girl provides the commentary as vignettes demonstrate that "far too many Swedes are sleeping badly". A stroppy man at breakfast searches for his glasses, which he's wearing. Girl "He's not slept well". Nor have lady who drops her handbag down refuse chute instead of the garbage, jogger who runs into lamp-post, a Mum who leaves with wrong baby from play park. Ends on our girl bouncing around in showroom full of the new range of Sultan beds, which Ikea have developed as the solution.

Forsman & Bodenfors, Gothenburg
CW: Fredrik Jansson
AD: Karin Jacobsson
AP: Magnus Kennhed / Charlotte Most

S/S Fladen, Stockholm
Dir: Måns Herngren
Prod: Patrick Ryborn

78a **FAKTA SUPERMARKETS** • Stay Longer — Denmark

Opens on typewriter title: "How to make the customer stay longer in a fakta shop". Added title: "Barcodes". At check out a young cashier reads out the barcodes line by line, item by item. "Thick, thick, thin, thin, thick". "Thin, thin, thick, medium-thin". This is filmed for real with a hidden camera so it is genuine fakta shoppers who look on in disbelief. One girl asks, "Do you have to say them all? ". fakta – "it only takes 5 minutes".

Uncle Grey, Aarhus
CD: Per Pedersen
CW: Thomas Falkenberg
AD: Jonas Nørregaard / Anders Tranæs
AP: Jan Pedersen

Lassie Film, Copenhagen
Dir: Jan Gleie
Prod: Stig Weiss

78b **FAKTA SUPERMARKETS** • Moving Goods — Denmark

Opens on typewriter title: "How to make the customer stay longer in a fakta shop". Added title: "Moving Goods". Filmed for real on hidden camera, so the confusion caused is with real fakta shoppers. Loudspeaker on: "This is fakta with information. The shoe polish is now next to the potato chips – which have been moved to the mayonnaise..." "Fruit and vegetables are above the baby food, except apples which..." Etc. One male shopper, in particular, with his list, is mesmerised and scratching his head. fakta. "It only takes 5 minutes".

Uncle Grey, Aarhus
CD: Per Pedersen
CW: Thomas Falkenberg
AD: Jonas Nørregaard / Anders Tranæs
AP: Jan P

Lassie Film, Copenhagen
Dir: Jan Gleie
Prod: Stig Weiss

79a CHICAGO MUSIC EXCHANGE • Smash — USA

In the Chicago Music Exchange store, a cool guy
in leather coat and jeans is trying a guitar. He can really
play. He finishes with some wild chords, a leap and
a gyrating arm. Two store clerks look on. The man then
smashes the guitar to smithereens and says, "I'll take it".
Store clerk says, "Good choice" and escorts him to the
till. Chicago Music Exchange. For the guitar obsessed.

Element 79, Chicago

CD: Danny Schuman
CW: Rick Hamman
AD: Matt Spett
AP: Craig Jelniker

Chelsea Pictures, New York

Dir: Evan Bernard
Prod: Jeremy Barrett

79b CHICAGO MUSIC EXCHANGE • Encore — USA

Two store assistants look on as a guy on a stool tries
out a guitar. He finishes his tune, replaces guitar, leaves
store. The two clerks clap politely, and their applause
develops into whooping and raucous cheering.
The customer comes back from pavement, waves them
to calm down, takes a guitar and plays again. Chicago
Music Exchange. For the guitar obsessed.

Element 79, Chicago

CD: Danny Schuman
CW: Rick Hamman
AD: Matt Spett
AP: Craig Jelniker

Chelsea Pictures, New York

Dir: Evan Bernard
Prod: Jeremy Barrett

80a **FEDEX/KINKO'S** • Shower — USA

Two white-collar guys enter the office washroom and join four others in a shower cubicle. "Sir, why are we meeting in the shower?" Boss: "My ideas always hit me in my shower at home and our first store opens next week. Any ideas?" One of them says, "FedEx/Kinko's for signs, banners, printing invitations, even shipping". Boss: "Wow, this shower thing really works". They leave shower laughing, a janitor looks on shocked. FedEx/Kinko's. Make it. Print it. Pack it. Ship it.

BBDO, New York
CD: Eric Silver
CW: Jim Lemaitre
AD: Jonathan Mackler
AP: Elise Greiche

Hungry Man, Santa Monica
Dir: Hank Perlman

80b **FEDEX/KINKO'S** • Plastic — USA

An employee helping a customer at a FedEx/Kinko's counter wears a plastic rain coat. He explains the Pack and Ship service, adding "And, I'll tell you what. If you use FedEx Ground, you ship for up to 34% less than at the UPS store". The customer splutters coffee all over the FedEx/Kinko's guy, who says, "It's ok. It happens all the time". The new FedEx/Kinko's. Make it. Print it. Pack it. Ship it.

BBDO, New York
CD: Eric Silver
CW: Jim Lemaitre
AD: Jonathan Mackler
AP: Elise Greiche

Hungry Man, Santa Monica
Dir: Hank Perlman

Wanting to do the best commercial on The Superbowl, FedEx/Kinko's did research and identified the top ten ingredients. 1. "Celebrity" – Burt Reynolds at a FedEx/Kinko's counter. 2. "Animal" – enter a grizzly bear. 3. "Dancing animal" – Reynolds and bear dance. 4. "Cute kid" – who says, "That bear can dance!" 5. "Groin kick" – which bear gives Reynolds. 6. "Talking animal" – bear apologies. 7. "Attractive females" – viz cheerleaders – "That bear can talk!" 8. "Product message (optional)" – delivered by Burt. 9. "Famous pop song" – over FedEx logo. 10. "Bonus ending" – bear to Burt – "I loved you in Smokey and the Bandit".

BBDO, New York
CD: Eric Silver
CW: Dan Kelleher
AD: Jerome Marucci
AP: Elise Greiche

Hungry Man, Santa Monica
Dir: Bryan Buckley

81a **ADIDAS** • Nadia

In this campaign the production magic is almost as much of a metaphor for "Impossible is Nothing" as the awesome athletic achievements relived. Here two 13-year-old girl gymnasts perform together on the high bar. One is current podigy, Nastia Luken. The other is the legendary Nadia Comaneci of 20 years ago. Nastia's voice under recalls how "Nadia was the first to show the world the perfect 10". Routine completed, the girls in turn execute triple somersault landings to the mat. Nadia gives Nastia a little nod of respect. Impossible is Nothing. adidas.

180 Amsterdam (180\TBWA)
CD: Peter McHugh (180) / Lee Clow (TBWA)
CW: Richard Bullock
AD: Dean Maryon
AP: Peter Cline / Cedric Gairard

Park Pictures, New York
Dir: Lance Acord
Prod: Jackie Kelman-Bisbee / Deannie O'Neil

81b **ADIDAS** • Jesse

Shot in black and white and opens at the 1936 Olympic Stadium in Berlin. Current world 100 metres champion Kim Collins recalls the immortal achievement of his hero and inspiration, four time Olympic Gold medal winner, Jesse Owens. Archive film of the Berlin 100 shows Owens powering ahead at 50 metres then seamlessly incorporates Kim Collins, who is the one to breast the tape. Owens and Collins pose grinningly together for the photographers. Impossible is Nothing. adidas.

180 Amsterdam (180\TBWA)
CD: Peter McHugh (180) / Lee Clow (TBWA)
CW: Richard Bullock
AD: Dean Maryon
AP: Peter Cline / Cedric Gairard

Park Pictures, New York
Dir: Lance Acord
Prod: Jackie Kelman-Bisbee / Deannie O'Neil

81c ADIDAS • Haile

Haile Gebrselassie, maybe the greatest runner of all time, asks, "How do I believe I can make myself keep going faster?" We realise it's not his competitors he raced to beat, or the clock, but something more personal, as we watch Haile - who broke his own world record 9 times - running a 10,000 metres race against 8 other magnificent athletes… who are all himself! "Impossible?", asks the winner, "Right. But you know I hate to lose". Impossible is Nothing. adidas.

180 Amsterdam (180\TBWA)
CD: Peter McHugh (180) / Lee Clow (TBWA)
CW: Richard Bullock
AD: Dean Maryon
AP: Peter Cline / Cedric Gairard

Park Pictures, New York
Dir: Lance Acord
Prod: Jackie Kelman-Bisbee / Deannie O'Neil

82 NIKE • Evolution

Open on close up shot of Nike's first basketball shoe. This magics into the Nike shoe that followed, with it's ankle-strap innovation. This magics into the next Nike basketball shoe with it's pull-back wings. The progression continues and the commercial illustrates the technology and unique features that characterised the construct and style of the seven key Nike basketball shoes from which the Huarache evolved. Air Zoom Huarache 2K4. Nikebasketball.com.

Wieden+Kennedy, Portland, OR
CD: Hal Curtis / Mike Byrne
CW: Jason Bagley
AD: Brad Irost
AP: Jennifer Fiske

The Embassy
Dir: Neill Blomkamp

83   TELECOM ITALIA • Gandhi   45th   Italy

Mahatma Gandhi sits cross-legged in his modest home making a speech. It's being filmed on a modern webcam. Cut to great screen in Times Square. A massive crowd in 1930's clothes and styles listens intently to his message of love. As do a young couple in Rome on a mobile phone; a native bushman on his laptop; a throng of 1930's Russians in Red Square. "Imagine the world today, if he could have communicated like this". Telecom Italia. Communication is life.

Y&R Italia, Milan
CD: Aldo Cernuto / Roberto Pizzigoni
CW: Marco Cremona
AD: Isabella Bernardi
AP: Gabriella Colombo

Colorado Film, Milan
Dir: Spike Lee
Prod: Fabrizio Don Vito / Marco Cohen

84a   ADIDAS • Hello Tomorrow   USA

adidas 1 is the first shoe with a computer. A young man wakes in blackness. His adidas lace themselves onto his feet and take him on a mysterious journey through inhospitable terrain. The darkness lights up in fragments. The world's first intelligent shoes enable him to turn gravity on its head in several directions, escaping a series of hairy situations, and get him safely back into his bed. It's a story of re-birth and taking your first steps again. Impossible Is Nothing. adidas.

TBWA\Chiat\Day (180\TBWA), San Francisco
CD: Lee Clow / Chuck McBride / Joe Kayser
CW: Chuck McBride
AD: Joe Kayser
AP: Jennifer Golub

MJZ, Los Angeles
Dir: Spike Jonze
Prod: Vincent Landay

84b **ADIDAS** • Made to Perfection   USA

God, who is black, is up in heaven carefully moulding, assembling and painting miniature basketball players. Next, as an awestruck janitor watches, God's giant hand rips the roof off a city stadium. And He places His dolls in a face off on the court and drops a basketball between them. As the ball bounces, the manikins, who are NBA legends Kevin Garnett, Tracy McGrady and Tim Duncan, come to life. Duncan grabs the ball and the game is on. Impossible Is Nothing. adidas.

TBWA\Chiat\Day (180\TBWA), San Francisco

CD: C McBride / S Duchon / J Patroulis / G Edwards
CW: Scott Duchon / John Patroulis
AD: Geoff Edwards
AP: Jennifer Golub / Andrea Bustabade

Omaha Pictures, Santa Monica

Dir: Rupert Sanders

85a/b **NIKE** • Popcorn / Telegraph Pole   China

A campaign of 15-seconders, shot with sports students, each featuring a small-town everyday event which turns into a sports opportunity. In "Popcorn", a young guy walking down the street stoops to tie his shoelace. There's an explosion noise from a nearby workshop. Young guy sprints off like an athlete from the blocks. In "Telegraph Pole", a hard hat guy up a pole has a bucket strapped to his back for his tools. A bunch of kids play street basketball using it as a hoop. Each spot ends with title over: "Anytime" and Nike swoosh.

JWT, Shanghai

CD: S Lo / B Chan / N Lim / H Gang / T Zhu
CW: Thomas Zhu / Joe Wu / Yin Xue Chun / Diana Li
AD: Hu Gang / Liang Hai / Paul Yu / Bamboo Zhuang
AP: Sandra Zhao

Perfect Life, Beijing

Dir: Li Wei Ran
Prod: Xie Zheng Yu

85c/d NIKE • Send Flowers / Bus Station   CHINA

A campaign of 15-seconders, shot with sports students, each featuring a small-town everyday event that turns into a sports opportunity. In "Send Flowers", a young man with bunch of flowers waits outside a building. His girlfriend comes out, he holds out flowers. She dispatches him over her shoulder in a karate throw. In "Bus Station", we get view from a bus of young man sprinting to catch it at the next stop. But as bus slows, another runner passes him a baton and he races off again. Each spot ends with title over: "Anytime" and Nike swoosh.

JWT, Shanghai
CD: S Lo / B Chan / N Lim / H Gang / T Zhu
CW: Thomas Zhu / Joe Wu / Yin Xue Chun / Diana Li
AD: Hu Gang / Liang Hai / Paul Yu / Bamboo Zhuang
AP: Sandra Zhao

Perfect Life, Beijing
Dir: Li Wei Ran
Prod: Xie Zheng Yu

85e/f NIKE • Late / Globe   CHINA

A campaign of 15-seconders, shot with sports students, each featuring a small-town everyday event that turns into a sports opportunity. In "Late", a student arrives in classroom late. The teacher scolds him and waves her pointer. He uses his umbrella and they have a fencing match. In "Globe", with teacher at blackboard, a globe rolls off its stand onto a pupil's desk. He grabs it and spins it on his finger like a basketball. Each spot ends with title over: "Anytime" and Nike swoosh.

JWT, Shanghai
CD: S Lo / B Chan / N Lim / H Gang / T Zhu
CW: Thomas Zhu / Joe Wu / Yin Xue Chun / Diana Li
AD: Hu Gang / Liang Hai / Paul Yu / Bamboo Zhuang
AP: Sandra Zhao

Perfect Life, Beijing
Dir: Li Wei Ran
Prod: Xie Zheng Yu

We're at opening scenes of Muhammad Ali's historic Sonny Liston fight in Zaire. But, when opponent's hood is thrown back – it's his daughter, Laila Ali (also a boxing champion today). Clever post-production pits them in a bruising bout in the packed stadium. Laila's internal monologue, "So when my father looks impossible in the eye and defeats it again and again, what do you think I'm gonna do when they say women shouldn't box?" She lands a solid punch. adidas. Impossible is Nothing.

180 Amsterdam (180\TBWA)
CD: Peter McHugh (180) / Lee Clow (TBWA)
CW: Richard Bullock
AD: Dean Maryon
AP: Peter Cline / Cedric Gairard

Park Pictures, New York
Dir: Lance Acord
Prod: Jackie Kelman-Bisbee / Deannie O'Neil

87 **NEXTEL** • Dance USA

Two white-collar guys are boogie-ing away in an office. Their boss enters, "What's going on here? We don't know how many converters we have in stock. We don't know where our trucks are. Nobody knows where Macklin is". Dancers stop. One punches his handset: "6000 converters". The other taps at a laptop, locating trucks precisely. The first raises speaker, "Macklin where are you?" "At the airport". Officer retreats; dancing resumes. "Inventory Management. GPS Services. Coast-to-coast walkie talkie". Nextel. Done.

TBWA\Chiat\Day, New York
CD: Gerry Graf
CW: Ian Reichenthal
AD: Scott Vitrone
AP: Nathy Aviram

Hungry Man, New York
Dir: Jim Jenkins

88a **SPRINT PCS** • Red Ball USA

A teacher is with her class out in a park. Each child has a red ball. Teacher: "OK. So everybody has their ball? What I need now is for you to tell me how many minutes you're going to use this ball every month. For the next 2 years". Poor kids scratch heads, try counting on fingers, look completely puzzled and perplexed. VO: "We need a better way to buy wireless". With the Sprint PCS Flexible Plan, the monthly rate adjusts to the minutes you actually use. Sprint PCS – "Now that's better".

Publicis & Hal Riney, San Francisco
CD: Erin Alvo / Mark Sweeney
CW: Mark Sweeney
AD: Erin Avlo
AP: Carolyn Casey

Non.Fic.Tion Spots, Santa Monica
Dir: Barbara Kopple
Prod: Michael Degan / Jim Shippee

88b SPRINT PCS • New Kid — USA

Opens on a school painting class. Teacher has a surprise for them – a new kid, Emily - and explains, "Since she's new, she gets the new deluxe paint set. It's got 40 colours of paint and crayons, brand new brushes and lots of sparkle, stars and glitter". Class looks less than happy re this – one asks why. Teacher, "Because she's new, which makes her special". At Sprint, existing customers can get great deals on the latest phones too. Sprint PCS – "Now that's better"

Publicis & Hal Riney, San Francisco
CD: Erin Alvo / Mark Sweeney
CW: Mark Sweeney
AD: Erin Avlo
AP: Carolyn Casey

Non.Fic.Tion Spots, Santa Monica
Dir: Barbara Kopple
Prod: Michael Degan / Jim Shippee

89a THAILAND YELLOW PAGES • Dad — Thailand

A young man, whose mother is dying, goes out to find the dad who deserted them – mom revealed he owns a tyre shop in Bochae market. Tearfully he confronts a man in a tyre shop: "I wouldn't even step in here if mom didn't ask!" The man's current wife and little girl witness the torrent of accusation. Until the man points out there are 3 tyre shops in Bochae market. Young man deflated, "Er, how much is that tyre?" He leaves. Better use Thailand Yellow Pages.

Creative Juice\G1 (TBWA), Bangkok
CD: Thirasak Tanapatanakul / Prangthip Praditpong
CW: Prangthip Praditpong /
        Nutchanun Chiaphanumas
AD: Thirasak Tanapatanakul / Jon Chalermwong /
        Kittitat Larppitakpong
AP: Jutharat Chingduang

Phenomena, Bangkok
Dir: Thanonchai Sornsrivichai

89b **THAILAND YELLOW PAGES** • Police Thailand

A macho man at home eats supper with his family. The phone rings. A voice: "Meng Jewellery? Mr Meng, listen to me. I have your son in my hands. Bring 10 million baht. Warehouse No 3, Klongtoen Pier". The man asks caller to repeat address and writes it down. Photos on wall reveal he is a champion police marksman. "Honey, where's my rifle?" he calls, pushing back his chair. "For the right data, call 1188". Thailand Yellow Pages.

Creative Juice\G1 (TBWA), Bangkok
CD: Thirasak Tanapatanakul
CW: Prangthip Praditpong /
        Nutchanun Chiaphanumas
AD: Thirasak Tanapatanakul / Jon Chalermwong /
        Kittitat Larppitakpong
AP: Jutharat Chingduang

Phenomena, Bangkok
Dir: Thanonchai Sornsrivichai

90a **VIRGIN MOBILE** • Shower USA

A black couple stand a few yards apart in the street. They sing a conversation to each other as if they were talking on phone in different locations. "Hello, yo, Mike. What y'doing?" "I just stepped out of the shower". "Are you naked?" "No, I'm not. I got my terry cloth robe on…" For the love of music – Virgin Mobile. Get free real music ring tones on the VOX 8610.

Fallon New York
CD: Ari Merkin
CW: Adam Alshin
AD: Marcus Woolcott
AP: Erika Best / Tammy Auel

MJZ, New York
Dir: Tom Kuntz / Mike Maguire
Prod: Jeff Scrunton

90b VIRGIN MOBILE • Thing   USA

A guy in brown shirt and jeans and a girl in pink top
and jeans stand apart on a street corner. They sing
a conversation to each other as if they were talking on
the phone in different locations. "Hello". "Hey, baby".
"Did you ever talk to him about that thing?"
"Chicken sounds delicious". "He's in the room isn't he?"
"Ye…es"… etc. For the love of music – Virgin Mobile.
Get free real music ring tones on the VOX 8610.

Fallon New York
CD: Ari Merkin
CW: Adam Alshin
AD: Marcus Woolcott
AP: Erika Best / Tammy Auel

MJZ, New York
Dir: Tom Kuntz / Mike Maguire
Prod: Jeff Scrunton

90c VIRGIN MOBILE • Call Waiting   USA

Two men stand on an empty pavement facing camera.
They sing a conversation to one another as if they were
on the phone in different locations. "Hullo". "Hey, Brian.
What you doin?" "No..oo.thing!" A woman steps into the
picture beside Brian – "Wait, let me get rid of this call.."
"Hello Brian" (the girl). "Baby, I can't talk right now".
Woman leaves the screen. For the love of music – Virgin
Mobile. Get free real music ring tones on the VOX 8610.

Fallon New York
CD: Ari Merkin
CW: Adam Alshin
AD: Marcus Woolcott
AP: Erika Best / Tammy Auel

MJZ, New York
Dir: Tom Kuntz / Mike Maguire
Prod: Jeff Scrunton

91a SFR MOBILE NETWORK • Star   France

One of the two "mecs" (the campaign characters) boarding a plane, espies French star Emmanuelle Beart asleep in business class. He takes seat next to her, lays his head beside hers, takes a photo on his phone and sends it to his mate. The guy then exposes Ms. Beart's lovely shoulder and leans in closer. Astonished mate rings him, which wakes the star, who finds a strange young man poised to kiss her. "You were snoring", our guy explains. With SFR Mobile you can instantly send photos. SFR. "Let's talk mobile".

Publicis Conseil, Paris
CD: Olivier Altmann
CW: Bruno Delhomme
AD: Andrea Leupold
AP: Jacques Fouché

Quad Productions, Paris / WAM, Boulogne-Billancourt
Dir: Rémy Belvaux
Prod: Nicolas Duval

91b SFR MOBILE NETWORK • Group   France

Vignettes portray "les deux mecs" (the campaign characters) relentlessly chatting up women. Seduction venues include the fitness club, an aerobics class, a pregnancy group with exercise balls, a swimming pool, a Tupperware party (yes, they even do that), a touchie-feelie yoga class, a ladies hairdressing salon. End scene, as they compare address books on their mobiles, reveals that one got 123 phone numbers, the other 141. SFR Mobiles hold up to 150 numbers. SFR. Let's talk mobile.

Publicis Conseil, Paris
CD: Olivier Altmann
CW: Bruno Delhomme
AD: Andrea Leupold
AP: Jacques Fouché

Quad Productions, Paris / WAM, Boulogne-Billancourt
Dir: Rémy Belvaux
Prod: Nicolas Duval

91c SFR MOBILE NETWORK • Analysis Laboratory   France

With much leering and winking to his mate, one of our "mecs" disappears into his apartment with a gorgeous girl. She pushes him back on the sofa, shirts are ripped off, she is starting on his zipper, when the landline rings. They ignore it, of course, so the answer machine picks up: "Yes, hello, this is Dr Baker. Your inflamed scrotum may be due to a genital bacteria…". The girl rolls away and starts to dress. With a mobile phone, personal calls really are personal. SFR. Let's talk mobile.

Publicis Conseil, Paris

CD: Olivier Altmann
CW: Guilhem Arnal
AD: Robin de Lestrade
AP: Jacques Fouché

Quad Productions, Paris / WAM, Boulogne-Billancourt

Dir: Rémy Belvaux
Prod: Nicolas Duval

92a ORANGE MOBILE NETWORK • Sean Astin   8th   Great Britain

The Orange Film Funding Board sits to hear a pitch from a top director – "Mr Astin, how do you follow 'Lord of the Rings'?" He wants to do something completely different – an epic romantic comedy set in New York. They'd prefer it to be in New Zealand, the fourth in the trilogy, "The Lord of The Ring Tones". Astin storms out in high dudgeon, leaving his sandwich, causing one mocking board member to mimic, "Hobbit, he's left the precious food". Don't let a Mobile Phone ruin your movie. Switch it off. Orange

Mother, London

CD: Mark Waites / Robert Saville
CW: Yan Elliott
AD: Luke Williamson
AP: Hayley Irow

Hungry Man, New York

Dir: Bryan Buckley
Prod: Kevin Byrne

92b ORANGE MOBILE NETWORK • Verne Troyer   8th   Great Britain

Verne Troyer (aka Mini Me) pitches his idea for a movie about misfits trying to find a voice in society. The Orange Film Funding Board are looking "for less wide screen, more phone screen". Exasperated, Verne pleads, "This film needs stature". "No, this film needs funding". A panel member then raises his little finger to his mouth and, imitating Dr Evil, says, "About one million English Pounds". Verne responds by giving them the finger. Don't let a mobile phone ruin your movie. Please switch it off.

Mother, London
CD: Mark Waites / Robert Saville
CW: Yan Elliott
AD: Luke Williamson
AP: Hayley Irow

Hungry Man, New York
Dir: Bryan Buckley
Prod: Kevin Byrne

92c ORANGE MOBILE NETWORK • Patrick Swayze   8th   Great Britain

"Patrick Swayze. Your film pitch please," the chairman of the Orange Film Funding Board briskly opens a session. P. Swayze, giving it all he's got, "I am a mute assassin on a trail of revenge. I will not speak until I find the killer of my mother". Whoa, right there, Patrick, silence doesn't exactly sell phones. "The Chatty Hunter" is put forward as a better title. Patrick Swayze stalks out in disbelief: the board are smug that they've weeded out a bummer. Don't let a Mobile Phone ruin your movie. Switch if off. Orange.

Mother, London
CD: Mark Waites / Robert Saville
CW: Yan Elliott
AD: Luke Williamson
AP: Hayley Irow

Hungry Man, New York
Dir: Bryan Buckley
Prod: Kevin Byrne

93 AUSTRALIAN RED CROSS • We Gave Blood   Australia

The Ad Agency Creative

The Producer

The Voice Over Artist

For this commercial, the agency team and the film crew rolled up their sleeves and were filmed donating blood. Nurses bustle efficiently, as camera shows a succession of individuals giving their blood. Titles over: "The director of this commercial" ... "The ad agency creative" …"The sound recordist" …"The producer"… The gaffer"…"The colour grader". Etc. Last to be shown – "The voice-over artist". He explains how Australia requires 20,000 blood donations a week. "So we gave our blood to make this ad".

BMF, Sydney
CD: Warren Brown
CW: Andrew Petch
AD: Andrew Ostrom
AP: Mandy Payne

Caravan Pictures, Sydney
Dir: Ben Lawrence
Prod: Emma Lawrence

94 INPES/PASSIVE SMOKING AWARENESS • Marie   17th   France

Camera travels slowly from room to room in a house. Each room is filled with huge heaps of cigarette butts. "Marie has smoked 22,430 cigarettes in the kitchen… 38,249 cigarettes in the living room…" Same is shown and enumerated for car and bedroom for a total of 142,740 cigarettes. VO: "That's a lot…" Cut to solemn little girl on a sofa with her teddy. "Considering she's 7-years-old". When you smoke, non-smokers smoke too. INPES.

FCB Paris, Clichy
CD: Thomas Stern
CW: Dominque Marchand
AD: Jean-Michel Alırol
AP: Suzanne Hormain

@radical.media, Paris
Dir: Les Elvis

95 NSPCC • Ventriloquist | 7th | **Great Britain**

Sally, an abused child, is portrayed as a ventriloquist's doll on her abuser's knee. Whenever she's asked a question – like what's nine times eight at school, or in the playground, "do you want to come round my place after school?" - the ventriloquist answers for her. At tea back home, "Sally, you're not eating", says her worried Mum. The ventriloquist, operating Sally's mouth, "I'm fine. Can I go now". Abused children can't speak up. Find out how you can help us be there for them. NSPCC.

Saatchi & Saatchi, London

CD: Tony Granger
CW: Leo Premutico
AD: Jan Jacobs
AP: Manuela Franzini

Large, London

Dir: Danny Kleinman
Prod: Johnnie Frankel

96a THAI HEALTH - ALCOHOL ABUSE • Sexual Harassment | 14th | **Thailand**

Two white collar guys in a pub. "Sales were slow last month," complains one. Two pretty girls sit down at the next table. Salesman gives each a sample of his product – a plastic fly swat. Cut to title: "2 hours later". Salesman is drunk and lurches over at girls… "Wanna go out with a real man?" They swipe him away with his own fly swats. Titles: "How Well Do You Handle Your Drinking?" "Think Before You Drink". Thai Health Promotion Foundation.

Saatchi & Saatchi, Bangkok

CD: Jureeporn Thaidumrong
CW: Prasert Vijitpawan / Krai Killikorn
AD: Supon Khaotong / Nuntawat Chaipornkaew
AP: Natee Wangtrakoon

Phenomena, Bangkok

Dir: Thanonchai Sornsrivichai
Prod: Piyawan Mungkung

96b THAI HEALTH - ALCOHOL ABUSE • Bar Fight 14th Thailand

Two young guys enter a pub. They order and proceed to super glue their table to the floor and wrap foam pads around their bottles. Cut to title: "3 Hours Later". The lads have become raucous and are banging and singing. A customer asks them to "Keep it down", which is their cue for a fight. But no tables get over-turned or bottles smashed, thanks to their earlier precautions. "How Well Do You Handle Your Drinking?" "Think Before You Drink". Thai Health Promotion Foundation.

Saatchi & Saatchi, Bangkok
CD: Jureeporn Thaidumrong
CW: Prasert Vijitpawan / Krai Kittikorn
AD: Supon Khaotong / Nuntawat Chaipornkaew
AP: Natee Wangtrakoon

Phenomena, Bangkok
Dir: Thanonchai Sornsrivichai
Prod: Piyawan Mungkung

96c THAI HEALTH - DRINK DRIVING • Response 14th Thailand

Title: "When you get drunk, your responses take longer". We see a drunk in a pub as his bottle of whisky rolls off table. Crash. 3 seconds later he grabs for bottle. Canned laughter. Waiter brings change. Man grabs for it well after waiter has taken it back believing it to be his tip. Canned laughter. Etc. Finally, he's driving car with a glazed look. He hits a child, who flies through air like a rag doll. Cut back to driver. And, before he responds, cut to title: "Don't Drive Drunk."

Saatchi & Saatchi, Bangkok
CD: Jureeporn Thaidumrong
CW: Prasert Vijitpawan / Krai Kittikorn
AD: Supon Khaotong / Nuntawat Chaipornkaew
AP: Natee Wangtrakoon

Phenomena, Bangkok
Dir: Thanonchai Sornsrivichai
Prod: Piyawan Mungkung

97a DFT/DEPARTMENT FOR TRANSPORTATION • Lucky — Great Britain

 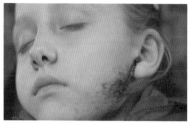 

We see a dead girl lying against a tree at the roadside. Child's voice: "If you hit me at 40 m.p.h., there's an 80% chance I will die". Slowly the child's injuries are reversed: the trickle of blood flows back into her ear and her body slides back into the middle of the road. Where she sits up with a gasp. "Hit me at 30 and there is around an 80% chance that I'll live". Title over: "It's 30 for a reason". Think!

Abbott Mead Vickers.BBDO, London
CD: Paul Belfor / Nigel Roberts
CW: Mary Wear
AD: Andy McKay
AP: Trish Russell

Academy Films, London
Dir: Walter Stern
Prod: Laura Kaufman

97b DFT/DEPARTMENT FOR TRANSPORTATION • Crash — Great Britain

Two guys at table in a pub as mate brings over another round. One of them protests, "Already 'ad one, I'm driving, 'int I?" His mates: "And?". Meanwhile, the one who's driving and an attractive young woman at the bar have been exchanging glances. She approaches, and suddenly we hear screeching brakes. The girl's head smashes into the table and she's thrown back limp and bloodied against the bar. VO: "It takes less than you might think to become a drunk driver". Think!

Leo Burnett, London
CD: Jim Thornton
CW: Angus MacAdam / Paul Jordan
AD: Angus MacAdam / Paul Jordan
AP: Emma Bewley

Small Family Business, London
Dir: Ringan Ledwidge
Prod: Sally Humphries

98   UNICEF/JUVENILE JUSTICE LAW REFORM • Bunso   The Philippines

A 13-year-old inmate, Tony, gives camera a tour of "the minors' quarter" in a Philippines jail. (A title has told us: "Over 10,000 children are detained each year. Most of them are in adult jails"). Tony shows us the sleeping quarters – each inch of floor space taken… the toilet… the shit bucket. The commercial calls for support to the passage of the Comprehensive Juvenile Justice Law. End title reads: "Unfortunately for Tony it's too late. He died last year. In detention".

BBDO Guerrero Ortega, Makati City
CD: David Guerrero
CW: David Guerrero
AD: David Ferrer
AP: Jeng Floresca

Ditsi Carolino, Quezon City
Dir: Ditsi Carolino

99   MEXICAN RED CROSS • Ambulance   Mexico

A red car speeds through the city late at night. Teenagers inside are whooping and hollering and standing up through the sunroof. Car enters a tunnel, screeches round a bend, we hear a crash. Title: "You can always count on the Red Cross". Cut to a Red Cross ambulance getting a call. They're on their way – medics prepare in back. They enter a tunnel too. Crash! Title: "But can the Red Cross count on you?" Cut to wrecked red car and ambulance at the scene of their collision. Red Cross. 2005 National Fund Raising Campaign.

Nazca Saatchi & Saatchi Mexico, Mexico City
CD: Jose Arce
CW: Marco Ochoa / Jose Arce
AD: Pascual Garciá
AP: Marcelo Genel

Central Films, Mexico City
Dir: Rodrigo Garcia
Prod: Diego Dopasso

100a **AMERICAN LEGACY FOUNDATION** • Drill   40th   USA

An event staged in New York City "outside a major tobacco company". Girl with megaphone: "This is my friend, Joannie. Her dad was a loyal customer of this tobacco company". They sent him a drill when he retired and a card (copies handed to spectators) – "Congratulations you're a winner". Joannie's dad had died of lung cancer three years earlier. She takes the megaphone to ask: "Why do you sell a product that kills your customers?" Ask questions. Seek truth.

Arnold Worldwide, Boston / Crispin Porter + Bogusky, Miami
CD: R Lawner / P Favat / A Bogusky / J Kearse / T Adams
CW: Megarock / John Kearse
AD: Brandon Sides / Phil Covitz
AP: Carron Pedonti

Redtree Productions, Boston
Dir: Christian Hoagland
Prod: Jeff Trenner

100b **AMERICAN LEGACY FOUNDATION** • Voice   40th   USA

Reportage coverage in the street "outside a major tobacco company". Podium with mike has been erected and behind it a vintage Virginia Slims poster. Girl announces: "Tobacco companies have been targeting women for the last 70 years, asking us to find our voice". She brings on her friend Grace, who's had her larynx removed and speaks with mike to throat: "Is this the voice you expected me to find?" Ask questions. Seek truth.

Arnold Worldwide, Boston / Crispin Porter + Bogusky, Miami
CD: R Lawner / P Favat / A Bogusky / J Kearse / T Adams
CW: Jackie Hathiramani
AD: Tricia Ting
AP: Carron Pedonti

Redtree Productions, Boston
Dir: Christian Hoagland
Prod: Jeff Trenner

100c AMERICAN LEGACY FOUNDATION • Flag | 40th | USA

A procession through the streets of NYC to a tobacco company's building. A flagpole is erected – beside the company's flagpole. The stars and stripes is run up. Half-way up. Young man with megaphone aimed at building: "When there's a tragedy American fly flags at half mast". So he has a question out of respect for the 1200 people killed by tobacco companies' products every day: "Are you thinking of lowering your flag?" Ask questions. Seek truth.

Arnold Worldwide, Boston / Crispin Porter + Bogusky, Miami

CD: R Lawner / P Favat / A Bogusky / J Kearse / T Adams
CW: John Kearse
AD: Phil Covitz
AP: Carron Pedonti

Redtree Productions, Boston

Dir: Christian Hoagland
Prod: Jeff Trenner

101 ORGAN TRANSPLANTS ASSOCIATION • Kitchen | Brazil

We open on a housewife at kitchen sink washing dishes. A glass in the foreground suddenly scrapes across the counter in her direction. The glass moves again. The woman stops and stares. The glass makes a bigger move: the woman retreats from kitchen. Super: "If you want to donate your organs, tell your family now". Woman has peek round door. "Later they may not understand you". ABTO. Organ Transplants Association.

DDB Brasil, Sao Paulo

CD: Sergio Valente / Pedro Cappeletti
CW: Miguel Bemfica
AD: Mariana Sa
AP: Luiz Filipe Fratino / Gilberto Pires / Jaqueline Couto

Caradecao Filmes, Rio de Janeiro

Dir: Rene Sampaio
Prod: Cris Amorim

102a THAI ENERGY POLICY & PLANNING OFFICE • Oil Price 34th Thailand

A customer at a gas station rudely complains about the price – 21 Baht a litre. "Are you selling your Mom's pussy?" Campaign character, Mr Energy intervenes. Sticking a lime in the nasty man's mouth, Mr E asks the pump attendant the price of a litre in England, Hong Kong and neighbouring Laos and Cambodia. Answers: 82, 69, 34 and 32 Baht respectively. Ends on set piece where Mr Energy, the pump attendant and male customer raise clenched fists against the sky. "Help your country save energy".

Saatchi & Saatchi Thailand, Bangkok
CD: Jureeporn Thaidumrong
CW: Wiparat Nantananontchai
AD: Thana Rittirajcomporn ; Tawatchai Suknipitapong
AP: Natee Wangtrakoon

Phenomena, Bangkok
Dir: Thanonchai Sornsrivichai
Prod: Piyawan Mungkung

102b THAI ENERGY POLICY & PLANNING OFFICE • Lost Money 34th Thailand

A customer at a gas station bemoans the money he's spending. Mr Energy (campaign character) intervenes to show him the cause: a punk who's revving the engine of his huge truck with belching chimney stack exhaust pipes. "Our money (from the oil price absorption fund) has gone to cover the waste caused by these gas guzzlers". The customer leaps in cab of truck and beats up punk. Ends on set piece – Mr Energy, punk and customer raise clenched fists. "Help your country save energy".

Saatchi & Saatchi Thailand, Bangkok
CD: Jureeporn Thaidumrong
CW: Wiparat Nantananontchai
AD: Thana Rittirajcomporn; Tawatchai Suknipitapong
AP: Natee Wangtrakoon

Phenomena, Bangkok
Dir: Thanonchai Sornsrivichai
Prod: Piyawan Mungkung

102c THAI ENERGY POLICY & PLANNING OFFICE • Madam | 34th | Thailand

As a rich woman filling up complains about the price of gas, Mr Energy (campaign character) intervenes. He thanks her in advance for helping her country, then tells her how she can. "No excess baggage". Opening the boot of her car, he whistles. Locals from café flock across and empty trunk of huge load of shopping and valuables. Ends on set piece as Mr E raises clenched fist to sky. Madam reluctantly joins him. "Help your country save energy".

Saatchi & Saatchi Thailand, Bangkok
CD: Jureeporn Thaidumrong
CW: Wiparat Nantananontchai
AD: Thana Rittirajcomporn ; Tawatchai Suknipitapong
AP: Natee Wangtrakoon

Phenomena, Bangkok
Dir: Thanonchai Sornsrivichai
Prod: Piyawan Mungkung

103 AMNESTY INTERNATIONAL • Babies | Portugal

Opens on hospital nurse at her table reading magazine. Clock shows 2.20. Faint sound of baby crying off. Cut to newborns ward, with rows of cots. One little guy is wailing in his crib. Nurse reads on. Back in ward, a second baby joins in. And another. Soon the whole lot are squawking their tiny lungs out. Nurse abandons her magazine and goes to ward to rock and soothe the babies. Title on black: "Together we're stronger," Amnesty International. You can make a difference.

Euro RSCG Lisbon
CD: Pedro Bexiga / Marcelo Lourenço
CW: Marcelo Lourenço
AD: Pedro Bexiga / Marcelo Lourenço
AP: Viviane Casto

Show Off, Lisbon
Dir: Rita Nunes
Prod: Isabel Zuzarte

104 PONLE CORAZON / CHILDREN'S CANCER APPEAL• Magic 23rd Peru

Shot in black and white – a magician performs for passers-by in a park. Passing his hat around, he spots a young girl with her mother. He brings her forward and removes her hat, revealing she has no hair. The crowd is hushed as he places his own hat on the child's head and waves his wand. He raises the hat: the joyful child finds she has a healthy growth of shiny black hair. Super: "The magic of giving". Ponle Corazon.
Peruvian Children's Cancer Appeal.

Leo Burnett del Peru, Lima
CD: Juan Carlos Gómez de la Torre
CW: Juan Carlos Gómez de la Torre
AD: Beatriz Caravedo / Alvar Ramos
AP: Katy Klauer

7 Samurai, Lima
Dir: Tito Köster / Alvaro Velarde
Prod: Gabriela del Prado / Lorena Ugarteche

105 AIDES AWARENESS • Vibrators France

Cut to Vibrators song "Baby, Baby", cartoon film shows the growing up years of a young woman. As a schoolgirl she's teased by boys. Then she discovers the opposite sex and has a string of dating catastrophes. A first lover who stubs out his cigarette on her cartoon heart … a closet sado-masochist … a ski instructor for whom she requires a microscope … a black dude whose condom size is XXX. Before finally she meets the man of her dreams. "Live long enough to find the right one". Aides. Protect yourself.

TBWA\Paris, Boulogne-Billancourt
CD: Erik Vervroegen
CW: Véronique Sels / Erik Vervroegen
AD: Erik Vervroegen
AP: Christine Bouffort

Wanda Productions, La Plaine Saint-Denis
Dir: Wilfrid Brimo

THE SHOWREEL OF THE YEAR 2005 INDEX

Alcoholic Beverages

1	**Smirnoff** • Diamond	Great Britain
2	**Fernet Cinzano** • Statistic	Argentina
3	**San Miguel/Reina Beer** • Carnival	Spain
4a	**Guinness Extra Cold** • Surfer	Great Britain
4b	**Guinness Extra Cold** • Anticipation	Great Britain
4c	**Guinness Extra Cold** • Snail	Great Britain

Non-Alcoholic Beverages

5a	**Mountain Dew** • Hallway	USA
5b	**Mountain Dew** • Helicopter	USA
5c	**Mountain Dew** • Canopy	USA
6	**Coca-Cola** • Rivalries	Argentina
7a	**K-Fee Caffeine Drink** • Car	Germany
7b	**K-Fee Caffeine Drink** • Golf	Germany
7c	**K-Fee Caffeine Drink** • Beach	Germany
8	**Pepsi** • Surf	Brazil

Food

9	**Californian Milk Processor Board** • Russian Family	USA
10	**Charal Beef** • The Race	France
11	**Marmite** • The Blob	Great Britain
12	**Australian Meat & Livestock Commission** • Unaustralian	Australia

Confectionery & Snacks

13a	**Altoids Sours** • People of Pain	USA
13b	**Altoids Sours** • Mastering The Mother Tongue	USA
13c	**Altoids Sours** • Fable of The Fruit Bat	USA
14	**Kims Crisps** • Mix Up	Norway
15a	**Skittles Gum** • Shelter	Great Britain
15b	**Skittles Gum** • Cerubs	Great Britain

Home Maintenance & Supplies

16	**Energiser Batteries** • Manos Japonesa	USA
17	**Poliflor Furniture Polish** • Wind	Brazil
18	**Showbound Naturals** • Ping Pong	USA
19	**Whiskas Cat Food** • Scratches	Brazil

Toiletries & Cosmetics

20a	**Axe Body Spray** • Residue	USA
20b	**Axe Shower Gel** • Bath	USA
20c	**Axe Shower Gel** • Pipe	USA
21	**Rexona For Men** • Stunt City	Great Britain
22a	**Rexona Dry Deodorant** • Shirt	Argentina
22b	**Axe Body Spray** • No	Argentina
23	**Lynx 24-7** • Getting Dressed	Great Britain

Medicines & Pharmacy

24a	**Pampers** • Stairs	Argentina
24b	**Pampers** • Crying	Argentina
25	**Scotch Essence of Chicken** • Date	Thailand
26a	**Viagra** • Golf	Canada
26b	**Viagra** • Office	Canada
26c	**Viagra** • Coach	Canada

THE SHOWREEL OF THE YEAR 2005 INDEX

THE SHOWREEL OF THE YEAR 2005 INDEX

THE SHOWREEL OF THE YEAR 2005 INDEX

THE GUNN REPORT

The Most Awarded Print

2005

Frog

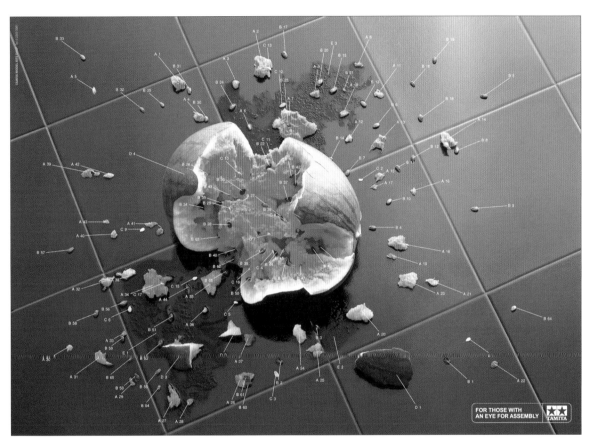

Watermelon

Light bulb

Creative Juice\G1, Bangkok

CD: Thirasak Tanapatanakul / Prangthip Praditpong
CW: Nutchanun Chiaphanumas
AD: Thirasak Tanapatanakul / Kittitat Larppitakpong / Jon Chalermwong
Photo: Anuchai Secharunputong / Nok

Churchill

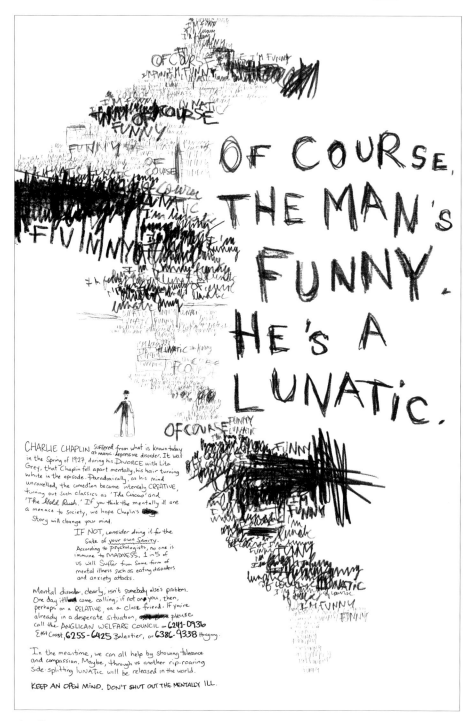

Chaplin

ANGLICAN WELFARE COUNCIL

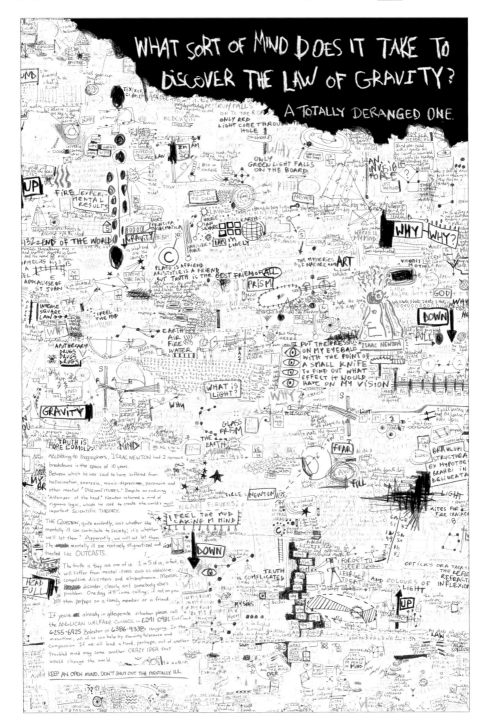

Newton

Ogilvy & Mather, Singapore

CD: Tham Khai Meng / Eugene Cheong
CW: Eugene Cheong
AD: Tham Khai Meng / Claire Chen
Illus: Agathe de Bailliencourt

VOLKSWAGEN POLO 3rd **Great Britain**

Small but tough. Polo.

King Kong

DDB London

CD: Jeremy Craigen / Ewan Paterson
CW: Simon Veksner
AD: Nick Allsop
Illus: Paul Slater
Typo: Kevin Clarke

BISLEY OFFICE EQUIPMENT | 4th | Germany

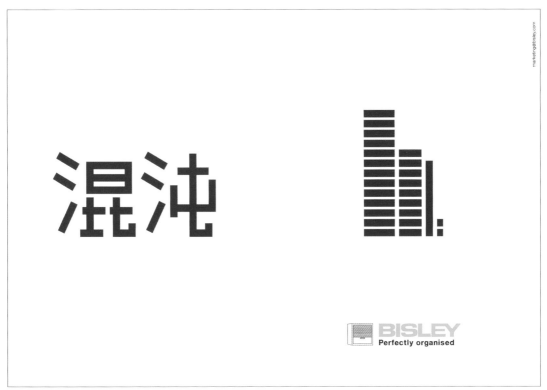

Chaos

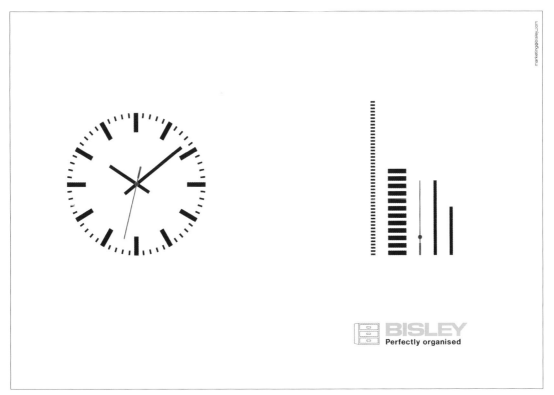

Clock

BISLEY OFFICE EQUIPMENT — 4th — Germany

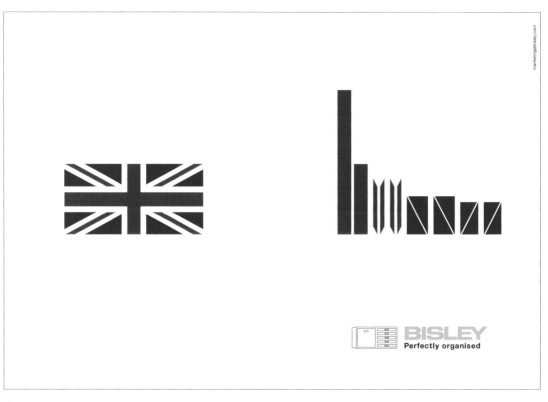

Flag

Kolle Rebbe Werbeagentur, Hamburg
CD: Andreas Geyer / Ulrich Zünkeller / Ursus Wehrli
CW: Klaus Huber
AD: James cè Cruickshank
Photo: James cè Cruickshank
Typo: James cè Cruickshank

Angola

Brazil

Columbia

USA

FCB Portugal, Lisbon

CD: Luis Silva Dias / Duarte Pinheiro de Melo
CW: Icaro Dória
AD: João Roque

THE ECONOMIST

6th **Great Britain**

Light Bulb

Abbott Mead Vickers.BBDO, London

CD: Paul Bedford / Nigel Roberts
CW: Nigel Roberts
AD: Paul Belford

ADIDAS 7th Japan

Impossible Sprint

TBWA\Tokyo

CD: John Merrifield
CW: John Merrifield
AD: Hirofumi Nakajima / Shintaro Hashimoto

Pizza Hut **PART OF HOME-MOVIES.** FOR DELIVERY CALL 62-35-35-35.

Singin' In The Rain

PIZZA HUT DELIVERY | 8th | **Singapore**

Psycho

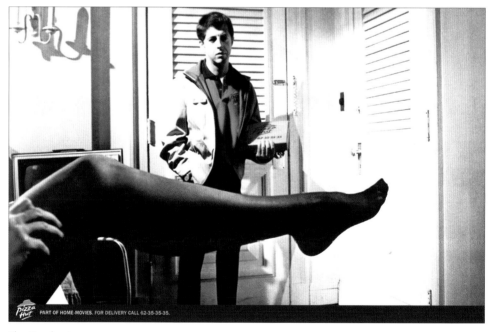

The Graduate

BBDO Singapore

CD: Francis Wee
CW: Ali Shabaz / Alex Lim Thye Aun
AD: Alex Lim Thye Aun / Ali Shabez
Photo: Teo / Nick
Illus: Sin Eng Lee
Typo: Alex Lim Thye Aun

Pendulum

Fallon, New York

CD:　Ari Merkin
CW:　Marty Senn
AD:　Molly Sheahan
Photo:　Steve Liss / Paula Bronstein

WERU NOISE PROTECTION WINDOWS

10th   Germany

Dogs

Garbage Collection

weru
soundproof windows

Rocker

Scholz & Friends, Berlin

CD: Jan Leube / Matthias Spaetgens
CW: Michael Haeussler
AD: Kay Leubke
Photo: Ralph Baiker

Exam Cheat Note

NUGGET SHOE POLISH 11th **South Africa**

Police Officer

The Jupiter Drawing Room, Johannesburg
CD: Graham Warsop
CW: Michael Blore
AD: Liam Wielopolski
Photo: Michael Meyersfeld

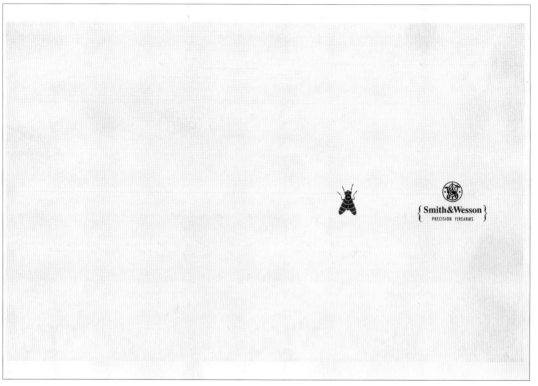

Fly

Bug

SMITH & WESSON 12th Germany

Moth

Springer & Jacoby, Hamburg
CD: Bettina Olf / Timm Weber
CW: Menno Kluin
AD: Menno Kluin
Illus: Joanna Switowski
Photo: Patrice Lange
Typo: Menno Kluin

11 NEWS 1 CHANNEL 13th Thailand

Boy

Businessman

11 NEWS 1 CHANNEL 13th Thailand

Housewife

Euro RSCG Flagship, Bangkok

ECD: Wiboon Leepakpreeda / Passapol Limpisirisan
CW: Nucharat Nuntananonchai / Passapol Limpisirisan
AD: Taya Sutthinun / Wiboor Leepakpreeda
Photo: Surat Jariyawattanawijit

Jayne Eyre

CZECH NATIONAL LIBRARY

Crime and Punishment

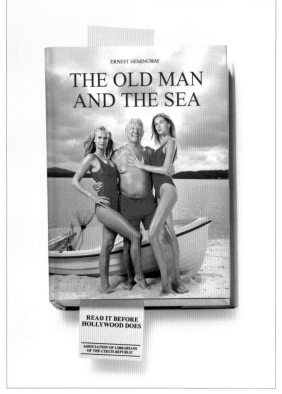

The Old Man and the Sea

Leo Burnett, Prague

CD: Basil Mina
CW: Mike Yee
AD: Mike Martin
Photo: Nikola & Goran Tacevski

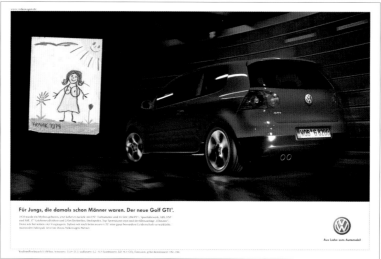

VOLKSWAGEN GOLF GTI | 15th | Germany

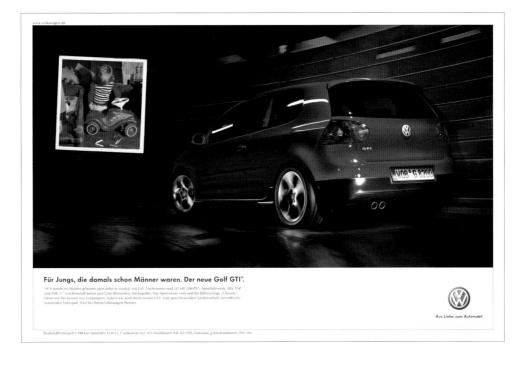

For Boys Who Were Always Men

DDB Germany, Berlin

CD: Amir Kassaei / Wolfgang Schneider / Mathias Stiller
CW: Ulrich Leutzenkirchen / Ilja Schmuschkowitsch
AD: Sandra Schilling
Photo: F. A. Cesar
Illus: Djamila Rabenstein

THE AKATU INSTITUTE FOR CONSCIOUS CONSUMPTION · 16th · Brazil

Favela

Leo Burnett, Sao Paulo

CD: Ruy Lindenberg
CW: Marcio Juniot
AD: Marcus Kauramura
Photo: Mario Daloia

SONY PLAYSTATION 2 17th France

Adultery

TBWA\Paris

CD: Erik Vervroegen
CW: Benoît Leroux
AD: Philippe Taroux
Photo: Dimitri Daniloff

VEJA MAGAZINE   18th   Brazil

Bin Laden

Bush

Saddam

AlmapBBDO, Sao Paulo

CD: Marcello Serpa
CW: Sophie Schoeburg
AD: Roberto Fernandez
Illus: Roberto Fernandez
Typo: José Roberto Bezerra

BIC PERMANENT MARKER 19th France

Old Lady

TBWA\Paris
CD: Erik Vervoegen
CW: Guillaume Chifflot
AD: Cedric Moutaud
Photo: Eric Matheron-Balay

Corridor

Fuse

AQUENT BUSINESS SERVICES | 20th | **Singapore**

Video

Coffee

Leo Burnett Singapore

CD: Linda Locke / Steve Straw / Tay Guan Hin
CW: Priti Kapur
AD: Goh Wee Kim
Diglm: Felix Wang
Photo: Ric Tang

THE GUNN REPORT

Guest Essays

2005

Michael Conrad

A blueprint for better work in your hands.

A few years ago the agency I was working for - as its worldwide chief creative officer - made it right to the top of table 8 "The Top 20 Networks in the World" in The Gunn Report. During the 5 years leading to 2001 over two dozen of our agencies were named "Agency of the Year" in their countries at least once. And 27 of the agencies around the network took home at least one Lion from Cannes.

Remembering those years I'm very proud of the many colleagues around the world whose thoughts on what constitutes 'better work' were placed on the same page and from there has been converted into good practice.

Now the many aspects and contents of the book you have in your hands can function as a blueprint to great advertising and is similar to what we initiated at Leo Burnett. If you're interested, here we go.

First of all we produced clear evidence that the big awards, won at major festivals, did beat non-awarded work in the marketplace, which is a no-brainer to most of the good people in advertising. But we wanted to stop those in our agency who were against the value of great awards and we also needed facts to convince and engage our clients.

We conducted four pieces of research over almost two decades under the headline "Does Award-Winning Advertising Sell? ". It delivered two major findings. About 80% of the work achieved or over-achieved on the goals set (60% of it was later awarded an Effi) whereas (in good times) the rule of thumb is that brands are either growing, flat or declining about 1/3 in each case. Secondly, some of those brands that won several awards over several years emerged as leaders in their categories.

Now, in digging deeper into the distinct merits of the work constituting this report "passion" and "focus" for good work became better defined, channelled and conceptualized which took us beyond evaluating the "good, the bad, the ugly" pushing the good for better and killing the bad and the ugly.
The term "bad and the ugly" was translated into more definable dimensions like "cliché", "pointless", "non competitive", "destructive"and "appalling". The "good" was defined as "setting a new standard in the category or in all advertising" creating visual and or verbal ownership for a brand, a point of difference, and beyond this pushing for Leo Burnett's demand for high end, "the best in the world, bar none".

In order to promote the high end and killing low end we wanted the work to fulfil three criteria, "innovative strategy", "fresh ideas" and "excellence in craft".

And importantly, because those standards were cultural-neutral, market-neutral, solution-neutral, media-neutral and free of rules, it worked out and was supported around the different nature of markets and clients globally, focusing on content, not on style.

Once we knew and agreed what quality we wanted, we began to manage it. Every quarter we took a whole week to evaluate the work against the above criteria, between 1000 and 1200 pieces, learnt from it, gave feedback to the makers and pushed ideas and initiatives for improvement. Interestingly this key meeting at Leo Burnett was started by my friend Donald Gunn. It was never ever cancelled or postponed and became an engaging, effective tool for quality management.

Another surprising fact sits in the middle of this report: over the years there is little change to the people, agencies and advertisers who are making the charts and leading the creative output of our industry. This means those making the charts have a very distinct way of working paired with endless energy and motivation to achieve something surprising and special. From the insights I have, 6 distinct areas of leadership emerge, areas those individuals in particular are extremely good at (which will also lay the foundation for the curriculum at the Berlin School of Creative Leadership).
Those areas cover "leading the enterprise", "leading the product", "leading the client", "leading the people", "leading one self" and "leading the industry".

I think our industry has reached a point where creative leadership has to be pushed by placing the creative forces at the centre of each universe. It seems to me most urgent to re-engage our audiences with advertising, eliminating the reasons why they use digital solutions to have their lives advertising free. We need to do everything we can to make them want to see the work we do again and again. Most of the work that is praised in the Gunn Report fulfils these criteria; most films have been emailed by people to their friend's computer, some of it by the millions.

We need an industry where the people involved are proud to be a part of it...and hot to get in.

Michael Conrad

MICHAEL CONRAD

In 1968 Michael began writing copy at Y&R Frankfurt.
In 1970 he moved to O&M Frankfurt and got promoted
to creative director in 1971.
In 1972 he co-founded TBWA Frankfurt.
In 1975 he co-founded with his friend Walter Lürzer
the Lürzer,Conrad agency
In 1980 the agency was merged with Leo Burnett
and renamed Michael Conrad & Leo Burnett in 1986.
In 1986 Michael moved to Chicago, working as president
and chief creative officer of Leo Burnett, International.
In 1997 Michael was named vice-chairman and chief
creative officer of Leo Burnett, Worldwide.
Michael retired in 2003 and lives with his wife Helga
in Zürich.

Michael is now helping to establish "The Berlin School
of Creative Leadership", a global project of the ADC Germany.
He is the Dean of the Roger Hatchuel Academy
at the "Cannes" International Advertising Festival.
He is member of the Board of Governors at the School
of the Art Institute, Chicago.

Michael chaired juries of prominent advertising festivals
around the globe, is honorary member of the ADC Germany,
ADC Switzerland and of the ADC*Europe.

Craig Davis • JWT

Let's keep dancing when the music stops...

Some words or phrases we hear have an impact that far outlasts the time they take to say. Nice things like "It's a boy", "We'd like to offer you a job", "I love you". Nasty things like "I'm afraid she passed away", "You're fired", "I'm leaving".

The communication doesn't stop the moment the sentence ends. Far from it, the words are just the tip of the iceberg – or the ears of the hippopotamus – depending on which continent you're sitting. It's not a monologue. But the start of a dialogue or conversation.

It's not just words that stand this particular test of time. The article you rip out of the newspaper to read again later. The toy or video game that lasts from one birthday to the next. The song or album you listen to on repeat. The TV series or movie you want to own on DVD for the extras. The web address you bookmark as a favourite, so often will you want to re-visit.

These are the communications that occupy the land beyond the now; the land where a 30 second advertisement isn't a success simply because it lasts 30 seconds, it's successful because it engages the audience longer than the duration of the message. Well into the 31st second and beyond.

Like a TV commercial that we choose to imitate to our friends over a drink. Like a radio ad we might find ourselves humming later that day. Like a magazine ad that instantly makes us want to rip it out and pin it to our office wall. Or visit the relevant website and play with the idea for a while. Maybe even interact with it and add to it. The kinds of ideas that can actually make time spent with advertising, time well spent.

It's important to remember, we are not just competing with every other bit of advertising communication, but with every message that bombards our audience. The average person is confronted by over 3500 messages every day. From spam emails to washing instructions. A trip to the supermarket can involve exposure to 1600 different messages – from parking instructions to information on the products themselves. Sifting out what's interesting from the banal has become second nature to our information-overloaded generation.

If you wonder why, dwell on these rather overwhelming facts.

Over half a million tonnes of rubbish thrown out in the UK alone last year was made up of 'junk' mail. More than

enough to fill the Millennium Dome a few times over. The average US household now receives 340 pounds of the stuff through the letterbox each year. Americans are now targeted by 817 TV commercials a week. Only to be outdone by Indonesians who are exposed to 852. New Zealanders are forced to endure an average of 12 minutes of advertising an hour.

When everyone is yelling and selling at you, begging for your attention, no wonder we switch over in a blink. There are now more media channels than ever to flirt with. In China, it will soon be possible to view 2000 TV stations via satellite. In Australia, over 65% of the population over 16 have mobile phones. In New York, nearly 80% of the population have computers at home, most with broadband access.

While all these media channels and entertainment offerings expand, people don't have any additional time to engage with them. 60 hours a week is about the limit, which is why the Internet business sees itself, quite literally, as "stealing time".

Time is increasingly in short supply.

Theophrastus, a Greek philosopher, was remarkably far sighted when he said, "Time is the most valuable thing one can spend". Time is at a premium.

As more people have more and more discretion in how they use the time available to them, every activity has become, in a sense, a competitor to every other. And given that advertising has to compete with this reality, in which the audience quite frankly has better things to do, it is important to re-evaluate what type of ideas are really worthy of people's time. If we are to compete in this new land, we need to change our focus.

We're not selling products. We're buying people's time.

Our ideas cannot just sit there and expect anyone's attention. Our ideas need to be those that provoke deeper, richer, more valuable involvement. Our ideas need to contribute to the audience's personal bottom line. Where they don't just get value for money, but value for time and an emotional return on the time they invest.

In essence, an idea that isn't worthy of anyone's time is frankly a waste of everyone's time. Instead, let's create ideas that people choose to spend time with.

Craig Davis • JWT

CRAIG DAVIS
Chief Creative Officer
JWT Worldwide

Craig Davis was appointed Chief Creative Officer of JWT's global network in January 2005. He joined JWT in March 2004 as Chief Creative Officer for JWT EMEA. He was previously at Saatchi and Saatchi where he was Regional Executive Creative Director for Asia/Africa. He held that position for the past four years. Between 1999 and 2000, he was Executive Creative Director of Saatchi's in Singapore. During his time in Asia, Craig was instrumental in driving Saatchi's to the number one creative network in the region. In 2002, Ad Age Global named him as one of the "Top 100 Advertising People" for his "dynamism, creativity, innovation, daring and leadership." In February 2004 Campaign Brief Asia, named him "Advertising Person of the Year." Davis's own work as a creative director and writer has been repeatedly recognised at Cannes, D&AD, the One Show, Clio and The Gunn Report.

John Hegarty • Bartle Bogle Hegarty

Despite everything one reads in the press about our business, this is the best time ever to be in advertising. Why? Because there is so much opportunity and possibility. Of course it's a period of great flux. But it is in moments of great change that great opportunity arises. Those who have courage and vision will be the ones that capture this exciting future.

It does of course require us to have a point of view on how best, in this changing environment, we can go on adding value to our clients business. This is about being proactive not reactive.

We constantly read that one of the threats to our industry is the consumer's power and their ability to switch us off. Be it with technology or just the sheer volume of advertising. Power has shifted to the consumer. We have to remind ourselves that this is called democracy. Not surely something we should be afraid of?

You can't read an article about advertising that doesn't in some way or another speculate that it's threatened by extinction if it doesn't do something to thwart this technological advance. This is the thinking of people who still believe in the advertising world of the 50's. A world where structures were firmly established and creativity took a back seat. And naturally in these times of doubt, the doom and gloom merchants are having a field day.

Why we should be so frightened by consumer empowerment bemuses me. What is truly amazing is that we now have even more ways of reaching the consumer. This has to be a cause for celebration. Not panic. We mustn't fall into the trap the music industry has collapsed into.

Believing that downloading, in other words greater access, is a threat. Making unlimited music available to an almost unlimited public should surely be cause for joy. What the music industry should be putting all their efforts into is working out how you make money out of this phenomena. Not stopping people doing it. Most brands fight for greater distribution not resist it.

The only threat to advertising is the paucity of interesting, engaging work. Work that is founded on a simple thing called, a great idea.

I find it incredible that as an industry we don't realize that our future will only be guaranteed if we deliver a better product. Just as GM has to make better cars to succeed. Vodafone has to provide better service to

succeed and your local grocery store has to provide more choice to succeed.

So we have to deliver a better product to succeed.

We cannot possibly believe that our future will be ensured by our ability to continually trick people into consuming our work. It won't.

Drumming repetitive, boring messages into peoples' brains is both unaffordable and ineffective. That's yesterday's thinking. More than that it's last century's thinking.

We must all know that we've moved from the era of interruption to one of engagement. People will just switch off the things that don't inspire them, involve them, and entertain them. This applies to movies, TV, books, and magazines as well as advertising.

The biggest threat to our industry isn't TIVO it's the quality of our product. And lets be honest, 90% of it is utter crap!

The first book was produced in about the 5th century AD. You know what, people are still reading them. But only if they're good.

How on earth do we think we can guarantee our future with a product people actively dislike. It's a salutary experience to go to a cinema in the US that shows ads. The audience, more often than not, starts booing. Not a healthy reaction to the product we produce. Nor one that will encourage talented people to join the business.

The fact that we have new ways of reaching people won't solve this problem. The problem will only be solved if we use those means of reaching people in a way that enriches their lives.

That has to be the greatest opportunity for the business of advertising.

I have found throughout my career, having worked with literally hundreds of brands. That whenever they get into trouble the surest way out is to make their product better.

And so it is with our business.

And of course technology can be a spur to creativity. As it has always been.

Yes there's product placement, break bumpers and branded entertainment. And of course the internet with viral messages. All these are great and we should be pursuing them with passion and inventiveness. But even

John Hegarty • Bartle Bogle Hegarty

here if they're not executed brilliantly they're not going to be effective. People don't read books because they're printed on glossy hand made paper. They read them because they capture the imagination.

You don't need a crystal ball to understand the future. There's no great mystery to it. You just have to make a better product. And remember, the greatest medium still is and always will be, word of mouth. Influencing that is our primary function. Those that embrace that challenge will be the ones that inherit the future.

JOHN HEGARTY
Chairman & Worldwide Creative Director
BBH

John started in advertising as a junior Art Director at Benton and Bowles, London in 1965. He almost finished in advertising 18 months later, when they fired him. He joined a small Soho agency, John Collings & Partners, going places. They did - out of town.

In 1967 he joined the Cramer Saatchi consultancy which became Saatchi & Saatchi in 1970, where he was a founding shareholder. One year later he was appointed Deputy Creative Director.

John left in 1973 to co-found TBWA, London as Creative Director. The agency was the first to be voted Campaigns (the UKs leading advertising magazine), Agency of the Year in 1980.

In 1982 he left to start Bartle Bogle Hegarty which was soon to become one of the most talked about advertising agencies in the World. Four years later, in 1986, BBH was voted Campaign magazine's Agency of the Year, and won the title again in 1993, 2003 and 2004. In addition, BBH became the Cannes Advertising Festivals very first Agency of the Year in 1993 by winning more awards than any other agency. It also won the title again in 1994. Most recently, BBH Worldwide was voted Campaign magazine's first ever Network of the Year at the end of 2004. BBH was also Campaign's Agency of the Year in 2003 and 2004.

In the first two decades of BBH's history, John was responsible for famous campaigns for Levi's® such as the famous "Laundrette" commercial starring an unknown model called Nick Kamen. He introduced the phrase 'Vorsprung Durch Technik' for Audi which has become one of the UK's most famous advertising slogans. He was the first to pick a young model/actor called Brad Pitt to star in a commercial and he also pioneered the importance of music for Levi's®. The result being the soundtracks from seven Levi's® commercials getting to the UK number one spot.

BBH has grown from being an agency in one location to "one agency in five places" with the opening of BBH Singapore in 1996, BBH New York 1998, BBH Tokyo in 1999 and most recently, a partnership with Brazillian hotshop agency Neogama in San Paolo. John now oversees the creative output of all BBH offices around the world. This unique global structure also contributed to the company winning the Queen's Award for Export Achievement twice, in 1996 and 1997.

Since setting up BBH, John's industry awards include two D&AD Golds and six Silvers, Cannes Golds and Silvers, and British Television Gold and Silvers. He was awarded the D&AD President's Award for outstanding achievement in the advertising industry and chaired the 1999 New York Art Directors Advertising Show. He has also been voted as one of the most influential people in fashion. And the International Clio Awards awarded John in May 2005, with the highly prestigious Life Time Achievement award for his outstanding achievement in the industry.

John regularly appears in the press and broadcast media as a spokesperson for the advertising industry and writes an occasional column on advertising in the UK's national Guardian newspaper.

SAATCHI & SAATCHI
NEW DIRECTORS' SHOWCASE 2005.

The Saatchi & Saatchi New Directors' Showcase is the best-attended event at Cannes apart from the Gala Award nights.

The popularity of the Showcase probably lies in its expect-the-unexpected reputation.

This applies to both the content of the reel and to the event we create around the screening.

The theme for this year's event sprang from the fact that the best directors distinguish themselves with their uniquely personal vision. And the impact this has on the audience's own vision.

So our invitation had a queasy-inducing shot of a hypodermic needle plunged into a beautiful model's eye.

On the Grand Auditorium stage, a spooky dance of 46 giant eyes represented the 23 directors we featured.

As always, the Showcase was an eclectic mix. A vivid round up of the world's hottest new directing talent.

The Showcase's track record for spotlighting outstanding talent now goes back 15 years. Tarsem, Jonathan Glazer, Michel Gondry, Danny Kleinman, Mark Romanek, Spike Jonze, Chris Cunningham and Ivan Zacharias are some of the people we've featured.

Paul Arden had the original idea for the Showcase when he was ECD of our London office. So, as a finale, I introduced Paul, who emerged from an enormous eyeball.

When Paul presented the first Showcase in 1991, the audience booed the work of Tarsem and Danny Kleinman. Paul stopped the screening and accused the audience of having "tin eyes". Fortunately, the audience now is much more receptive to new ideas.

If you're a new director yourself and you'd like to be considered for the 16th Saatchi & Saatchi New Directors' Showcase in 2006, the conditions are straightforward.

You should not have been directing commercials for more than two years.
You may have directed no commercials at all. But you have to be available to direct them now.
You can submit short films, animation, music promos. Anything that moves basically.

And of course, your work has to stand out amongst the initial 500 or so submissions sourced by our offices around the world. Having a unique vision will help enormously.

Bob Isherwood. Worldwide Creative Director. Saatchi & Saatchi.

If you're really interested in learning more about the Saatchi & Saatchi New Directors' Showcase, please email christian.goonan@saatchi.co.uk

Matt ASELTON
EPOCH FILMS

Michael DOWNING
HARVEST

Gaëlle DENIS
PASSION PICTURES

Chris NELSON
ANNEX FILMS

Oury ATLAN
PARTIZAN LAB

TOKYOPLASTIC
PICASSO PICTURES

NE-O
STINK

UGLY
UGLY PICTURES

Woof WAN-BAU
NEXUS PRODUCTIONS LTD

Mateus DE PAULA SANTOS
LOBO

HONEST
CZAR.US

Frank DEVOS
QUAD PRODUCTIONS

Joseph KOSINSKI
ANONYMOUS CONTENT

Associates IN SCIENCE
PARTIZAN

Randy KRALLMAN
HSI PRODUCTIONS, INC.

Eric HILLENBRAND
TEMPOMEDIA FILMPRODUCTION

Marcus TOMLINSON
@RADICAL.MEDIA

Baptiste MASSÉ
MILK ELEMENTARY RESOURCES PH

Andy FOGWILL & Agustin ALBERDI
LANDIA

Brett FORAKER
4CREATIVE

Adam SMITH
RSA FILMS

Kezia BARNETT
THE SWEET SHOP

Luciano PODCAMINSKY
PIONEER PRODUCTIONS

Bob Isherwood • Saatchi & Saatchi

BOB ISHERWOOD
Worldwide Creative Director,
Saatchi & Saatchi

Bob Isherwood was one of the first Australians to head north. Not to back-pack round Europe, but to pursue a career in advertising.

In London, after 6 years at Y&R, Bob then spent 10 very heady years at CDP. Surrounded by some of the world's most talented writers and art directors (and creative directors and account handlers and producers), Bob held his own. He kick started the Stella Artois "Reassuringly Expensive" campaign, for example.

He won Australia's first Gold Lion for Cinema at Cannes. He was the first Australian to win that rarest of honours, a British D&AD Gold. And he won the first ever D&AD Silver for Advertising Typography.

Bob's scheduled two year trip north lasted a little longer. 18 years and 10 months later he headed back to Australia to become a founding partner in Sydney's Campaign Palace.

4 years later he finally got it right when, in 1986, he joined Saatchi & Saatchi.

He became Worldwide Creative Director in 1996.

Bob believes passionately in the power of ideas to change the world. Appropriately, he is the driving force behind the Saatchi & Saatchi Award for World Changing Ideas.

He's also passionate about nurturing new talent. Maybe it's because he's something of a pioneer himself. It certainly explains why the impact of the New Directors' Showcase means so much to him.

Tham Khai Meng • Ogilvy & Mather

The Rise and Fall of Creative Stars

Imagine if you took one of those thermal imaging devices and adapted it to record creative heat. Then you scanned the Asia-Pacific region. What do you suppose you would see?

I imagine you would find two bright red blips amidst a sea of pallid blue, with here and there some blobs of purple.

The two red-hot spots would be Singapore and Bangkok. The purple areas would be the emerging or declining creative centres of Asia Pacific.

Some of the rising stars would be Tokyo, Auckland and Kuala Lumpur. (And Mumbai if we want to stretch it.)

At the other end of the spectrum are Melbourne, Sydney and Hong Kong: erstwhile luminaries whose flames have, alas, dimmed with the passage of time.

(This evaluation is based on performance in the international and regional award arenas over the last five years.)

In this essay I want to speculate on how this situation arose.

It's fairly clear that all the cities in question have the financial means to import talented people in a sufficient quantity to affect their creative climate. In other words, they have the wherewithal to blaze just as brightly as the supernovae.

So what accounts for the difference?

I suspect it might be partly to do with the openness of the society to outside stimulus, the degree to which they are more inward- or outward-looking.

A large part of my job consists of persuading talented people to work (and stay working) in Ogilvy's 38 Asian offices. And during the course of my work I've noticed one thing time and time again. Good people can't really be bought.

They are usually volunteers, and almost never mercenaries. (Of course, money is important to them, but only as a mean of keeping score.)

The single consistent quality I detect among creative volunteers is that they want (surprise, surprise) to be creative, and they will move to places that permit them (surprise, surprise again) to be creative.

Or as Professor Arnold Wasserman said, "Creative people will go to where creative people are."

For example, everyone that I interview wants a job in Singapore or Thailand, and only the intrepid and world-weary are prepared to slug it out in Ho Chi Minh City or Guangzhou.

So why are Singapore and Bangkok such stellar cities?

Is it their history, or their culture, perhaps, that predisposes them to be inventive? The minerals in the water? Or the special blend of carcinogens in the air that causes synapses to fire more freely and profusely there? Or maybe something to do with genealogy?

No. I'm afraid Hitler was wrong: an inherently superior race, Aryan or otherwise, does not exist. The Thais and Singaporeans are no more inherently creative than Pygmies are inherently great high jumpers.

To see this you only have to consult a few award annuals from a few years ago. As recently as a decade and a half ago, both Singapore and Bangkok were perceived as creative backwaters. And yet within a few years these third-world expatriate retirement homes had fashioned themselves into creative Meccas.

I've watched it happen, and also witnessed Sydney's fall from grace as a creative centre and seen Auckland eclipsing the Aussies. I've watched the decline and fall of Hong Kong, seen Tokyo drift in and out of greatness, cheered Mumbai in its eternal struggle to enter the League of Luminaries, and recently, discovered signs of life in Kuala Lumpur.

A city's creative luminosity, I've come to believe, lies in its ability to incubate, attract and hang on to talent.

If you toured the creative departments of Singapore, for example, you'd find Americans, Australians, Canadians, Dutch, English, Filipinos, French, Germans, Hong Kongers, Indians, Irish, Jamaicans, Japanese, Malaysians, New Zealanders, Norwegians, Scots, South Africans, Swedes, Welsh, and, of course, the odd local like myself with our feet up our desks. (Am I working in the U.N.? I forget sometimes.)

Singapore is a mongrel community seething with diverse experiences and opposing points of view. Cross-fertilization and mutual stimulation is a matter of course here. With everyone bringing his or her own bundle of knowledge and skill set, the labour of "combinatory play" in the sticky, steamy city-state is eclectic and somewhat surreal.

Tham Khai Meng • Ogilvy & Mather

The confluence of trade routes, migrants, and clashing cultures with equally confusing ideologies has turned this far-eastern, melting pot into a bizarre cauldron of human soup. It could have been the Tower of Babel, if not for English: the 'world language' that allowed the country's work to be seen and noted globally. Even in The Gunn Report.

So contrary to Mark Twain's view, the East and the West met half a degree north of the Equator and the lads and lassies are getting along swimmingly.

Bangkok's story is not so clear-cut. But it is surely not insignificant that the chap who affected the trajectory of the entire Thai advertising industry is an Australian by the name of Barry Owen. The fact that a farang was allowed to enter the underbelly of the ad industry to perform radical hysterectomy speaks volume for the Thai's openness.

They are a clever people who are adept at blending other cultures into their own. Visit northern Thailand and you'll hear the upcountry tribal music, Luk Thung, being belted out with electric guitars and synthesizer. Like a peanut butter and ginseng smoothie: it's eastern, western, primeval and present-day all at once.

Although the language forms a formidable barrier to outsiders, it's never stopped the Thais from acquiring enough English to collaborate with the rest of the world. Thai-lish, on the other hand, gives them an inscrutable veneer, which allows them to keep the world at a distance. The Siamese have, in the process, emerged worldly, wise and irritatingly smooth.

Singapore and Bangkok are, quite evidently, open societies.

They are tolerant, inclusive places where rebels, oddballs, and other non-standard people regardless of race, creed and sexual preference are welcome. Because of their low barriers of entry for talent, they have grown to become the creative epicentres of Asia.

On the other hand, Sydney strikes me more as a clubby community, where the normal man, the man without eccentricity or genius, is most likely to succeed. Neither the defective, nor the genius, has room to develop his innate disposition in such an environment.

Whereas establishment London marginalised a pirate like Neil French, there was enough space in little Singapore for his genius to detonate and mushroom boundlessly. The intensity of the conflagration is still being felt in Asia today.

Whether it's the British Royalty, the Indian Mafia or the Chinese Triad, all cliques, ultimately, are suffocating and, in the end, life-threatening. They provide jobs for the boys by excluding new blood, new people and new ideas. By insulating themselves from the outside world, they are, in effect, applying a tourniquet around their own neck.

Hong Kong's spectacular flop as a creative hub, for instance, corresponded with its rejection of outside talent. After the handover in 1997, an ethnic cleansing of 'expat' creatives swept through the former British colony. After the Diaspora, the local mob took over. 'The City of Life' has been dying daily ever since.

The faltering of Mumbai as a creative force in recent time is due, I believe, to its self-sufficiency. Along with rapid growth, comes hubris. Mumbai must never be tempted to close its doors on the world. If it wants to shine on the global stage, all sorts of talent need to be persuaded to walk through its doors.

Tokyo should be pulling a 'Hungry? Nissin Noodles' out of its hat on a yearly basis. The size and sophistication of its market demands it. Instead, it waxes and wanes, and wanes and waxes, its creative power is predictable insofar as it is unpredictable.

In a study of the Japanese culture—one notorious for its fickleness towards outside influence—the psychologist Dean Keith Simonton found that "those periods in which Japan was receptive to alien influx were soon followed by periods of augmented creative activity."

No man is an island. Not even the second largest advertising market in the world.

The truth, as always, is simple. If we are to shine like stars, there are really only two things we need to do:

Be tolerant of strangers, and be intolerant of mediocrity

Tham Khai Meng • Ogilvy & Mather

THAM KHAI MENG,
Co-Chairman, Asia Pacific
Executive Regional Creative Director
Ogilvy & Mather Asia Pacific

Khai was listed by AdAge Global New York, 2002 as one of Global Power 100 most influential people in the communication business. For three consecutive years since 2001, he was voted by Campaign Brief Asia as the number one creative director in Asia Pacific, leading the top agency network in the region.

Khai has bagged gold awards at Cannes, The New York One Show, New York Clio, London International Advertising, Asia Pacific AdFest, Asian Advertising Awards and China CCTV Awards. He had the honour to judge all these award shows. In 2004, he was chairman of the jury at the Asia Pacific AdFest. He was the 2005 chairman of the jury at the New York Clio.

In 2002, Khai was elected to the Prime Minister's Economic Review Sub-Committee, a think tank charged with the task of remaking Singapore into a knowledge-based economy. Khai sits on the board of Singapore Government's National Arts Council, Arts Education Council and is Deputy Chairman of Design Council. He sits on the board of three Temasek Holdings companies: Singapore Ventures, Singapore Cruise Centre, and Singapore Expo.

He is author of the book, 'The Ugly Duckling - a cautionary tale of creativity in advertising', now published in English, Korean, Japanese and Mandarin.

He started his career with Leo Burnett, London, and moved to their headquarters in Chicago. In 1992, he made the move to Batey as Executive Creative Director, Singapore and Sydney. He joined Ogilvy & Mather in 1999 and sits on the Worldwide Creative Council. In January 2005, Khai was elected to the Ogilvy & Mather Worldwide board.

Khai holds a Bachelor of Arts (1st Class) from Central St Martin's, UK, and a Master of Arts (summa cum laude) in Film and history of art from the Royal College of Art, UK, under the British government (DES) scholarship.

Marcello Serpa • AlmapBBDO

Understanding a country's advertising is impossible without touching a little of its soul.

In the case of Brasil, it is important to look beyond the cliché soccer/sex/beach/samba/caipirinha. For such, I'm going to ask for you to bear with me a little for a brief explanation of the Brazilian DNA and how it defines how we live, how we love and how we create ads.

Everything began in 1485 in a meeting with a Portuguese client, King João II, refusing a concept presented by a Genovese freelancer, Christopher Columbus.

With his ego badly hurt for having had an idea refused by the greatest client at the time, he knocked on the competition's door, the Catholic Spanish kings. Ferdinand and Izabela then bought the campaign that promised a shortcut to India and its spices.

Well, it wasn't quite India that he discovered, but for the client, what counts is the result, and that the Americas promised. So much so, that the Portuguese decided to copy Columbus's strategy, and in 1500 they sent Pedro Alvares Cabral more toward the south, where he discovered Brazil.

Much later, with the Spanish crown having cash-flow problems, the British started taking hold of the Northern American part of the continent. As of that moment, two very distinct types of colonization defined the region's future and luck.

With one tickets in their hands, the Anglo-Saxons settlers sought land eager to begin a new life far from the problems in Europe. To reach success, they knew they had to PRODUCE wealth.

The Spaniards and the Portuguese regarded their colonies as great reservoirs of Gold and Silver. To be successful, they only had to EXTRACT wealth and return to Europe rich.

These two distinct ambitions determined the differences between the protestant Anglo-Saxon northern colonization and the Iberian-Catholic colonization of the South to this day.

Although the desire for instant wealth characterized both the Spanish and the Portuguese, there were differences in their treatment of the native Americans.

Whilst the Spaniards subjugated, with zero politically correctness, the highly developed Mayan, Aztec and Inca civilizations, the Portuguese in Brazil found, in an Indian population living in a tropical Eden, the utopia imagined by Rousseau.

So unlike the dry land of the Aztecs and the Incas' cold Andean mountains, in Brazil, they just needed to shake a tree and dozens of exotic fruits would come down enough to feed an army. We say in Brasil, if you eat an Papaya and spits the seeds on the ground, in tree weeks you are selling papayas in the market.

The Portuguese were enchanted by the lovely naked Indian women and, rather than kill, they preferred to sleep with them.

But incapable of enslaving people that didn't know the meaning of work, much less slave work, they decided to import labor for the mines and sugar cane plantations from the African colonies. Once again the Portuguese's hormones betrayed them.

This...what I might call "more magnanimous"....character in the area of Portuguese hormonal urges, is what finally formed the Brazilian people.

This is where, in this typically erotic environment free from the Northern Protestant Puritanism, the Indians, Portuguese, and later, Africans, Germans, Italians, Japanese were received with open arms and legs.

Although far from being the Shangri-la of races, Brazil must be the country with the smallest difference between them. We all have a bit of everyone, we are all Brazilians. Stripped of labels, without Japanese-Brazilians, Afro-Brazilians or Italian-Brazilians.

500 years old. In terms of history, a pre-teen whose acne is visible in the São Paulo street potholes. With all the doubts and anxieties typical of its age, it is simultaneously capable of creating things that only the children's uncommitted and free cheerfulness is capable of generating.

With an obstinate optimism capable of overcoming all bad news that permeates our newspapers, a very particular sense of humor was born. It is difficult for an event, person or even tragedy to go by without a joke. It is from this juvenile cheerfulness and implacable humor that advertising gets its fuel.

In the 80's, agencies such as DPZ and W/Brasil worked in a market closed to foreign brands and products. Open TV, as a mass vehicle, divulged soap operas and 100%-Brazilian music. Hence, this closed local brand environment was ideal for the formation of a typically Brazilian advertising language. Supported by the strength

Marcello Serpa • AlmapBBDO

of television, the advertisement reflected the lighthearted and mocking language of the streets and ended up transforming itself in yet another display of the Brazilian popular culture.

With the economic stagnation in the beginning of the 90's, the opening of the market arrived. With it, new international brands, a new competition model with which Brazilians were not used to and the key-word in the 90's: Globalization.

Our main national brands were Globalized so, the TV channels, the marketing directors.

Suddenly, our local color, which once was our main advantage, became a disadvantage. No one in the world speaks our Portuguese; neither do they understand why we laugh in front of a TV set or reading a magazine.

At agencies such as DM9, AlmapBBDO and F/Nazca, a revolution is gradually beginning in advertising language. The excess text starts making room to the art direction in magazines. The Art Directors stopped being the ad decorators of the 80's to begin synthesizing concepts in simple but impacting images. Text makes room for images that can be understood in Rio, Buenos Aires or Tokyo.

The films leave the "actor-talking-to-the-camera" scheme and start seeking new visual formats. But the rule still being: Keep it simple. (with the budgets we have, this is not a Philosophie, but a way to survive.)

Maybe I, as an Art Director, may be a suspect in issuing my visual opinions. I have always believed in the power of images and their capacity to touch the pupils.

But I am certain that the transformation of an extremely discursive advertising into a visual synthesis was undoubtedly the great change that made Brazilian advertising noticed throughout the world in the last few years.

Talking less, but making many eyes worldwide smile with our humor.

MARCELLO SERPA
Partner & Creative Director
AlmapBBDO

Marcello Serpa, 42, has been creative director at AlmapBBDO since 1993, when he became a partner in the agency beside Jos Luiz Madeira. In 2004, AlmapBBDO was the most awarded agency in the world, according to the Gunn Report. It was the first Latin agency to reach the top of the ranking. Marcello studied visual and graphic arts in Germany, where he worked at the agencies GGK and R.G. Wiesmeir, and is the most awarded art director in Brazil. Among others, his is the first Brazilian Grand Prix at the Cannes Festival, in 1993, and the first Gold Pencil in Brazil at the One Show. In 2004, he was elected Best Creative Director in Brazil and Spanish-Speaking Countries at the Argentine El Ojo de Iberoamrica festival for the sixth time. In 2000, he was the youngest president of the TV and Print jury at Cannes.

Mark Tutssel • Leo Burnett

You get a brief. You have an idea. Your next reaction? Ring Frank Budgen. Ring Daniel Kleinman. Ring Ivan Zacharias. And why not? They are masters of their craft. And who on earth wouldn't want to do a Grand Prix-winning spot like PlayStation "Mountain." Like John West "Bear." Or Stella Artois. But why do we always turn to film when there is a tremendous spectrum of possibilities out there today?

The vast palette of visual arts available to us is endless. It can help our communications break out of the cliché. It can help create a personality and distinct character for the brand. It can make ideas more memorable and, more importantly, more engaging, allowing both the creator and viewer to use their imagination and indulge in a world of fantasy or exaggeration.

Claymation. Animation. Photographic illustration. Animation layered over live action. Puppetry. The possibilities are endless, but they're virtually untapped by the advertising world. Why? Because few of us dare to be different. Few of us explore life beyond live action.

As the media world becomes more fractured and messages fight harder for attention, you have to stop viewers dead in their tracks, and grab them by the eyeballs. You have to promise and deliver entertainment.

Clients are moving beyond the 30-second commercial that viewers so often zap or ignore. They are looking for new ways to connect with the consumer. The Internet, cell phones, Internet video-they're looking for a higher quality conversation with their consumers.

So what does this mean for television?

Not much in the short term. Television is still a $70 billion business. And even as big advertisers like McDonald's shift budgets toward the Internet, spending at the four major U.S. television networks is expected to inch up two percent this year, to $16.8 billion.

But clearly the job has become a lot harder.

As you all know, the consumer is king. The "click and pick" generation has arrived. And they're not leaving anytime soon. TV's destiny lies in the hands of consumers, who aren't afraid to use their remote controls. With the advent of TiVo, they're editing brands out of their viewing repertoire. Today's DVR early adopters watch 60 percent of their TV from the hard drive and skip 92 percent of ads. If you don't think that's scary, you should.

As John Hegarty so passionately pointed out at the 2005 Clio Awards, the only way we're going to stop the skipping is to make our commercials fresh, interesting and engaging. Personally, I don't think people have lost their ability to watch TV ads. Instead, I think the industry has lost the ability to write great TV ads.

In North America alone last year, we made around 25,000 TV commercials. How many of those commercials are people actually talking about? How many of those commercials did people actually watch? More importantly, how many of those commercials dared to be different?

We have to find fresh, new, visually striking ways to capture consumers' attention—as well as their hearts and their minds. We have to reward them for spending their time with our advertising, treat them with intelligence and, above all, entertain them.

I believe the visual world offers a vast array of incredible styles to bring your ideas to life. Evian "Waterboy" from Euro RSCG/Paris was visually one of the freshest, most talked about Gold winners at 2004 award shows. It took a traditional art form and gave it a distinctive, modern twist.

These days, strong visual marketing is vital to the success of any company. We live in a visual world. A highly competitive, visual world. In this industry, we must always strive for originality. Not only originality in idea, but also in execution. I'm not advocating that animation is always the answer. Instead I'm asking you to realize all of the options out there.

I'm asking you to be bolder. I'm asking you to be original.

If our duty is to produce the most engaging, relevant work, no matter what the medium, then I believe that, now more than ever, we must make our ads stand out, and I would argue that animation can help us do just that.

Mark Tutssel • Leo Burnett

In 1991, claymation and the brilliance of Aardman Animations put the British Electricity Board on the map and gave the brand a character that broke the mould. It was loved by the nation and swept the award shows. Aardman eventually won three Oscars for their short films starring Wallace and Gromit.

Films like the ones featuring Wallace and Gromit are experiencing unprecedented success. In today's media saturated world, there's an increasing appetite for new and different visual styles. That makes animation sexier than it's ever been. Movies like "Shrek" have reinvigorated animated feature films at the box office. For example, "Shrek II" ranks as the third highest grossing film of all time, with U.S. domestic revenues totaling over $440 million. To put that into perspective, that's just $20 million shy of the number two highest grossing film of all time-"Star Wars."

More recently, movies like Pixar's "The Incredibles" have experienced unprecedented success. Brad Bird, the film's director says that, "Animation is about creating the illusion of life." But he reminds us that you can't create that illusion of life "if you don't have one." Just as we borrow from our lives when crafting the stories we tell in commercials, I encourage all of you to borrow from your lives when creating visual styles for your ads. TV shows like "The Simpsons" and movies like "Sin City" and "Sky Captain and the World of Tomorrow" continue to break production rules and push boundaries. Why can't our ads do the same?

Ultimately, today's trends in animation started with one person, the grand master, Walt Disney. Disney was a storyteller, a showman, a dreamer, a genius. During his 43-year Hollywood career, which spanned the development of the motion picture medium as a modern American art, Walt Disney and his product made a huge impact on the landscape of popular culture.

When talking about his craft, Disney said, "Animation offers a medium of story telling and visual entertainment which can bring pleasure and information to people of all ages everywhere in the world."

Bringing pleasure, information and entertainment to people of all ages—isn't that what advertising is all about? Even though we've experienced advancements in technology, Disney is timeless. I would argue that two-dimensional animation is as fresh today as it was when it was first invented.

Computer animation is the staple diet of video games, and we live in a video game culture. Gamers as a group are getting older. Today's average player is 29. That means more disposable income and a target we cannot ignore. They expect their ads to be as sophisticated as their games.

Nintendo's famed game designer Mr. Miyamoto grew up without a television set, so his sense of adventure and imagination was limited only to what his own mind could produce. He grew up to use his imagination in the world of electronic games, where he would eventually create some of the world's most recognizable video game characters, like Super Mario Brothers and Donkey Kong.

Mr. Miyamoto once said, "What if, on a crowded street, you look up and see something appear that should not, given what we know, be there. You either shake your head and dismiss it, or you accept that there is much more to the world than we think."

As Sir David Puttnam has said, "Like it or not we live in an age in which moving images pervade every aspect of our lives." Sometimes you cannot separate a brand from its visual style. The visual style becomes the brand's DNA. He suggests that advertising is at the heart of all of this. To him, "Strong visual marketing is increasingly vital to the success of any company or product—however great its

intrinsic merits may be. We're constantly being asked to buy into images, whether it be a political party or a new brand of lemonade." Or in the case of Diesel, fashion. Their internet film titled "I Fly Over Kitchen City" is nothing but images created by Pez without even a glimpse of the product.

Puttnam believes "commercials directors, like their counterparts in feature films, deal in heightened reality, a world comprised of artificial and deliberately attractive images. Both are in the seduction business. Both are looking to create visual images that steal up on you quietly, subtly winning you over, shifting your attitudes and working away at your emotions."

The best commercials beguile, inspire and entertain. Creating something that has genuine mass appeal. Commercials may not be the best possible medium for putting across complex ideas, but they can be unbelievably successful at creating a series of powerful, lasting images which linger in the viewer's mind long after many others have faded." Consider TBWA's Apple iPod campaign. Or MTV. I would argue that few brands know themselves like MTV. For almost 24 years, MTV has embraced animation and new visual styles to create a distinct tone of voice and personality for the brand. MTV doesn't follow trends, it creates them.

Another brand that has created a distinct tone of voice and personality is Honda. They believe in the power of dreams, and clearly the power of a big idea. "Grrr" is truly an unbelievable, magical piece of film, executed brilliantly, and unlike any car ad in history. The spot was six months in the making and holds your attention for every beautifully crafted second. What I personally love is the irony of using classic animation and an old-fashioned jingle to create the most modern, inspiring piece of work in the world this year.

So next time you get a brief, dare to be different. Step outside your comfort zone. If it's not scary, it's probably wrong.

That just might open the possibility of doing something as groundbreaking as Honda "Grrr".

Mark Tutssel • Leo Burnett

MARK TUTSSEL
Worldwide Deputy Chief Creative Officer
Leo Burnett

Mark Tutssel is one of the world's most awarded Creative Directors, and his work has garnered every major creative award in the industry, including the prestigious International Cannes Grand Prix and 22 Cannes Lions.

In 2002, Mark joined Leo Burnett USA as Vice Chairman/Deputy Chief Creative Officer with a brief to raise the creative profile of the flagship agency. Since then, he has overseen creative for clients, including Kellogg's, General Motors, McDonald's, Nintendo, Morgan Stanley, Beck's and Procter & Gamble. In 2004, the agency ranked No. 17 among the Gunn Report's "Most Awarded Agencies in the World."

In January 2005, Mark was promoted to his current position of Worldwide Deputy Chief Creative Officer. In his new position, he will be single-mindedly focused on big ideas that cross channels and time.

Prior to joining Leo Burnett USA, Mark served as Executive Creative Director of Leo Burnett London. Under his creative leadership, the London agency experienced unprecedented success, becoming the No. 1 creative agency in the United Kingdom and the most awarded agency in the world in 2001.

Mark also lends his creative expertise to the global advertising community. He has served as Chairman of the 2000 Eurobest Awards, the 2003 International YoungGuns Awards, the 2005 International Addy Awards and the 2005 Clio Awards Television Jury. He has also served as a jury member at Cannes and D&AD. In 2006, he will chair the International Andy Awards.

THE GUNN REP●RT

Student Competitions

2005

STUDENT COMPETITIONS

By Dr Patricia Alvey
Director, Temerlin Advertising Institute, SMU Dallas, TX

In its seventh year, The Gunn Report adds a new category. We begin featuring the most awarded advertising schools and student work. A key function in the life of The Gunn Report is to contribute to and support education: by enabling schools to be able to study the 100 most awarded commercials and campaigns in the world each year. And, via The Gunn Report Library@BEAM.tv (a remarkable teaching resource), to study the best commercials of all time.

Reciprocally, Donald, Emma and Mike at Festivals where they've participated in 2005, have been struck by the quality of the work in the Student sections and the high interest it generates in the industry. A case in point is the annual AAF conference (culmination of the ADDYs) where student and educator delegates are in equal number to those from agencies and those from advertisers.

With this addition of a student work section, we are able to support those industry competitions which include categories for aspiring advertising professionals, and take the logical next step to include student league tables and student Best of Show winners in the Showcase.

Adding this student section was a simple idea that became complicated as we reviewed the variety of competitions and showcases specific to students. Student competitions may use formats that are quite different from those in the professional arena. Some, for example, may create an assignment for entrants rather than making an open call for work. The primary types of student competitions or opportunities for visibility include:

magazine showcases;
agency pitch competitions;
on site/on demand competitions;
special assignment competitions; and
open "best work" competitions.

Our premier student section incorporates eight competitions from two of these categories: six globally recognized open competitions and two special assignment competitions that use judging criteria most similar to the open competitions.

The six competitions that most closely mirror professional competitions are: Addys, Andys, Athenas, Clios, New York Art Directors Club, and Young Guns Award. These competitions offer student categories that parallel the professional competitions in that students submit work they have created in the process of taking classes and assembling a portfolio. These are the open competitions and are the most easily reported. They are also most favored by educators because they allow students and faculty to showcase best work while making progress toward a completed portfolio. And, like agencies, best work for any school can be entered in multiple categories and competitions thereby accumulating accolades and notoriety akin to that of professional work.

The two competitions, included in this report, which create special assignments for students to solve are D&AD and The One Show. These competitions are formatted differently than the professional competitions showcased in The Gunn Report, but we've included them here because they have a legacy of excellence within the industry and student work is judged using quality parameters similar to the professional competitions.

Two categories of student competitions which we did not consider are the 'agency pitch' and the on site/on demand. The end product and the nature of judging agency pitches do not closely enough parallel the criteria reviewed in the professional competitions. The on site/on demand competitions also differ enough to exclude them from consideration.

In addition to reporting on global competitions which accept student work, we reviewed publications that regularly showcase student work. Lürzer's Int'l Archive publishes student work that is judged using professional criteria. The magazine CMYK shows only student work but uses a professional jury system for selection. Archive is in the process of selecting annual winning work and CMYK is considering the process.

STUDENT COMPETITIONS

Those may qualify as open submission competitions and would be considered for inclusion into the student tables in future years.

As the Student Competitions section in The Gunn Report matures, the number of competitions and the global scope are both going to broaden. To give a bit of a perspective, I've assembled for The Gunn Report records, a list of schools that have received consistent recognition of excellence in the past decade. Since this is mainly, not all, from a US-perspective, our task in the next 12 months will be to expand the list to reflect a truly comprehensive worldwide picture.

This year, in the Student Showcase, we are featuring the top award winners in each of the included eight competitions. We are not going in for "league tables" yet – until our data is closer to global. But, this would hardly be The Gunn Report if we didn't have a first stab at identifying some apparent star performers.

Most awarded Student Ads & Campaigns in 2005 (winners in 2+ of our 8 major competitions), in alphabetical order, are:

DHL Couriers "Houses"/"Skyscrapers"/"Factories"
Diet Coke "Tape Measure"/"Bottle Caps"/"Straws"
Laphroaig Malt Whisky "Woman"/"Hair"/"Brothers"
MagLite "Bright"
Play-Doh "Gorilla"/"Snake"/"Rhino"

Most awarded Advertising Schools & Colleges in 2005 – the USA and Global schools that were the biggest winners in our 8 competitions, in alphabetical order:

Academy of Art University (San Francisco)
Art Center of Design (Pasadena)
Miami Ad School (Hamburg)
Miami Ad School (Miami Beach)
Miami Ad School (Minneapolis)
Miami Ad School (San Francisco)
Portfolio Center (Atlanta)
School of Visual Arts (New York)
The Creative Circus (Atlanta)
VCU Adcenter (Richmond, VA)

And, recognizing that our first sample was highly US-biased, other **strongly performing non-US schools** (in addition to Miami Ad School, Hamburg) turned out to be:

AXIS Media & Design School (Auckland, NZ)
Buckingham Chilterns University College (UK)
Cambridge Regional College (UK)
Kingston College (UK)
RMIT University (Melbourne, Australia)
University of Applied Arts (Vienna, Austria)

In conclusion, this collection of excellent student work establishes a first benchmark for advertising educators and for those looking to recruit young professionals. We look forward to reviewing more international competitions and identifying those training grounds producing the best new creative talent - the future Gunn Report Leaders.

MIKE'S HARD LEMONADE • Heartbreaker   USA

At a minor league baseball game, a beautiful fan with a Mike's Hard Lemonade plays winky-wink with the Catcher, distracting him. The next pitch, a fastball speeds past the Catcher's glove, tears through his chest, and pops his heart out through his back. The animated heart jumps into the stands and wrestles the fan for her Mike's Hard Lemonade.

Addys • Best of Show TV

University of Southern California, L.A.
CW: Eric Badros
AD: Eric Badros
Dir: Eric Badros

PUMA • Grandpa   USA

A grey haired, bearded man is sitting in a chair in front of a window talking to a friend on the telephone about a crossword puzzle clue. A car pulls up outside and the man turns his head and sees it's his grandchildren. He ends the call. The children run into the house calling his name. Cut to a door at the rear of the house. It is open and no one is in sight. Super: Run. Puma.

Clios • TV Gold

Academy of Art University, San Francisco
CW: Sakib Affridi / Eric Larsen
AD: Sakib Affridi
Prod: Arlo Rosner
Dir: Arlo Rosner

ARIEL • Sky Tracker   USA

The campaign paired Ariel laundry detergent with the Wimbledon Championships, showing practising players illuminating the night sky with their tennis whites. The lights follow the sound design of each player as they move back and forth across the court. A guerrilla campaign brings the television spot to life by lighting up the London skyline with 16 spotlights for the entire length of the tournament.

D&AD • Gold - Open Brief Category

The Creative Circus, Atlanta
CW: Adam Kennedy / Brandon Rochon
AD: Adam Kennedy / Brandon Rochon

WASHINGTON STATE LOTTO · USA

File this

JEFF WEAVER, who ruthlessly dumped me, then tried to suck up to me after I won LOTTO, **LIVES RIGHT HERE.**

Jeff Weaver

Addys • Best of Show Print

School of Visual Concepts, Seattle
CW: J Brent Shrive
AD: Lara Papadakis

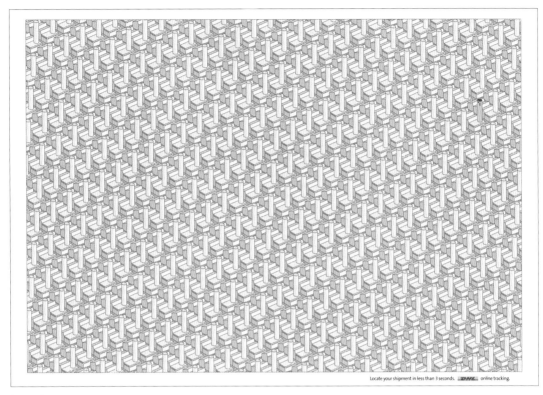

Factories

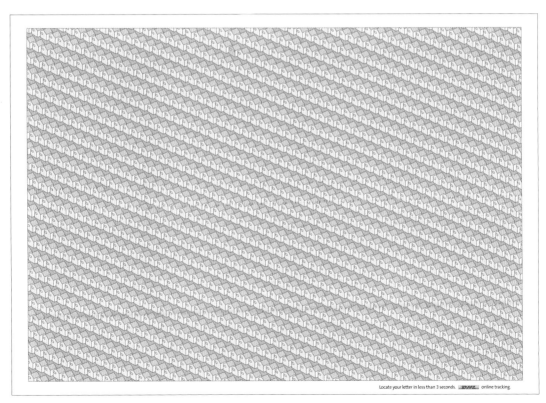

Houses

Skyscrapers

Andys • Glenn C Smith Student Silver

Miami Ad School Europe, Hamburg
CW:　Dylan Berg
AD:　Rune Degett

Fish

ODOR EATERS USA

Toilet

Athenas • Student Gold

Miami Ad School, Miami Beach

AD: Kevin Koller

HUBBA BUBBA   Germany

Orange

Pink

Clios • Print Gold

Miami Ad School Europe, Hamburg

CW: Menno Kluin
AD: Menno Kluin

227

MAGLITE   Germany

Bright

NYADC • Advertising Distinctive Merit

Miami Ad School Europe, Hamburg
CW: Patrick Herold
AD: Tim Zastera

DOMINO SUGAR   **USA**

Sweet 1

Sweet 1 - Detail

Sweet 2 - Detail

DOMINO SUGAR   **USA**

Sweet 2

Sweet 3

One Show • G College Competition Gold

Miami Ad School, Miami Beach
CW: Francisco Garcia-Tunon
AD: Michael Bae

PLAY DOH USA

Gorilla

Snake

PLAY-DOH   USA

Rhino

Young Guns • Student Winner

Miami Ad School, Minneapolis
CW: Matt Burgess
AD: Tom Zukoski

THE GUNN REPORT

Seven Year Consolidated Tables
1999-2005

2005

The Most Awarded TV Commercials and Campaigns in The World 1999 – 2005

			Ad pts	Year(s)
1	HONDA • Cog	Wieden+Kennedy (London)	45	03/04
2	SONY PLAYSTATION 2 • Mountain	TBWA\London	41	04/'05
3	HONDA DIESEL • Grrr	Wieden+Kennedy (London)	35	05
4	SOKEN DVD PLAYER • Plays Smoothly campaign	Euro RSCG Flagship (Bangkok)	34	04/'05
5	BUDWEISER • Whassup campaign	DDB Chicago	33	00/'01
6	JOHN WEST SALMON • Bear	Leo Burnett (London)	31	01/'02
7	THE INDEPENDENT • Litany	Lowe Howard-Spink (London)	30	99/'00
8	GUINNESS • Surfer	AMV.BBDO (London)	28	99/'00
9=	LEVI'S ENGINEERED JEANS • Twist	Bartle Bogle Hegarty (London)	27	01/'02
	NSPCC • Cartoon	Saatchi & Saatchi (London)	27	02/'03
11=	OUTPOST.COM • Band / Cannon / Forehead	Cliff Freeman & Partners (New York)	25	99
	REEBOK • Sofa	Lowe (London)	25	02/'03
13	QTV • Danster campaign	Mother (London)	24	01/'02
14=	ADIDAS • Laila	180 Amsterdam (180\TBWA)	23	04/'05
	FOX SPORTS TV/REGIONAL • campaign	Cliff Freeman & Partners (New York)	23	01/'02
	UNIF GREEN TEA • Worms	BBDO Bangkok	23	04/'05
17=	AXE DEODORANT SPRAY • Metamorphosis	VegaOlmosPonce (Buenos Aires)	22	02/'03
	EVIAN • Waterboy	BETC Euro RSCG (Paris)	22	04/'05
	FOX SPORTS TV/ML BASEBALL • Boat / Leaf Blower / Nail Gun	TBWA\Chiat\Day (San Francisco)	22	02/'03
	LYNX 24-7 • Getting Dressed	Bartle Bogle Hegarty (London)	22	04/'05
	PEUGEOT 206 • The Sculptor	Euro RSCG MCM (Milan)	22	03
	SONY PLAYSTATION • Double Life	TBWA\London	22	99
23=	GUINNESS • Bet on Black	AMV.BBDO (London)	21	00
	NIKE • Tag	Wieden+Kennedy (Portland, OR)	21	02
25=	AEROLINEAS ARGENTINAS • Shadow	JWT (Buenos Aires)	20	04/'05
	BUD LIGHT INSTITUTE • Greetings Cards / History	Downtown Partners DDB (Toronto)	20	03/04
	FOX SPORTS TV/NBA • Alan & Jerome campaign	Cliff Freeman & Partners (New York)	20	01
	JOHN SMITH'S BEER • Mum / Diving / Babies & campaign	TBWA\London	20	02/'03

The Most Awarded Print Ads and Campaigns in The World in 1999 – 2005

			Ad pts	Year(s)
1	VOLKSWAGEN / AFFORDABILITY • Wedding	BMP DDB (London)	31	99/'00
2	VOLKSWAGEN POLO • Cops	DDB London	30	04/'05
3	CLUB 18-30 HOLIDAYS • Bar / Beach / Pool	Saatchi & Saatchi (London)	27	02
4	BISLEY OFFICE EQUIPMENT • Perfectly Organised campaign	Kolle Rebbe (Hamburg)	22	04
5=	ADIDAS SOCCER • Vertical Football	TBWA\Japan (Tokyo)	21	04/'05
	SPHERE ACTION FIGURES • As Real As It Gets campaign	TBWA\Singapore	21	04/'05
7=	FEDEX • Box	BBDO (Bangkok)	20	01/'02
	TAMIYA MODEL KITS SHOP • Eye For Assembly campaign	Creative Juice/G1 (Bangkok)	20	05
	VEJA MAGAZINE • Get Both Sides campaign	AlmapBBDO (Sao Paulo)	20	04/'05
10	ANGLICAN WELFARE COUNCIL • Churchill / Chaplin / Newton	O&M Singapore	19	05
11	VOLKSWAGEN OF AMERICA • Hey, there's a... campaign	Arnold Worldwide (Boston)	17	01
12=	LEVI'S CLASSIC MEN'S 501's • Hugging & campaign	BBH (Singapore)	16	03
	NESTLE QUALITY STREET • Big Wrappers campaign	Lowe (London)	16	04/'05
	THE ECONOMIST • Brain	Ogilvy & Mather (Singapore)	16	04
	VIRGIN ATLANTIC • In Flight Channels campaign	Net#work BBDO (Jo'burg)	16	04/'05
	VOLKSWAGEN POLO • King Kong	DDB London	16	05
17=	DULUX PAINTS • Pregnant / Sunburn & campaign	Lowe Bull Calvert Pace (Jo'burg)	15	02
	GRANDE REPORTAGEM MAGAZINE • Flags campaign	FCB (Lisbon)	15	05
	GUINNESS EXTRA COLD • Lolly / Iceberg / Fan / Nipple & campaign	AMV.BBDO (London)	15	99/'01
	JOHN WEST TUNA • Fishing	Leo Burnett (London)	15	00/'01
	VOLKSWAGEN OF AMERICA/BEETLE RELAUNCH • Heart / Soul / Past Life / 0-60 & campaign	Arnold Worldwide (Boston)	15	99
	ZOO BUENOS AIRES • Giraffe / Polar Bear & campaign	Del Campo Nazca S&S (B. Aires)	15	03/'04
23=	CAMPAIGN BRIEF ASIA • Cecilia / Marc / Antoni	Saatchi & Saatchi (Hong Kong)	14	02
	CZECH NATIONAL LIBRARY • Hollywood Versions campaign	Leo Burnett (Prague)	14	04/'05
	SONY PLAYSTATION • Lara Croft	TBWA\Paris	14	00/'01
	VIRGINIA HOLOCAUST MUSEUM • campaign	The Martin Agency (Richmond, VA)	14	00
	VOLKSWAGEN BEETLE • Fun / Serious campaign	BMP DDB (London)	14	01

The Most Awarded Countries in The World 1999 – 2005

		Gunn Report Winner Points							
		1999	2000	2001	2002	2003	2004	2005	TOTAL
1	USA (1)	298	306	250	250	299	234	196	1833
2	Great Britain (3)	257	195	228	219	165	188	184	1436
3	Brazil (13)	110	94	89	71	79	81	80	604
4	Argentina (42)	76	61	81	70	93	81	94	556
5	France (5)	52	51	63	61	95	94	109	525
6	Spain (8)	89	77	103	76	67	62	47	521
7	Germany (4)	49	43	55	72	51	83	102	455
8	Thailand (27)	41	45	52	47	57	73	100	415
9	Japan (2)	46	50	59	53	38	55	57	358
10	Singapore (38)	49	35	41	38	43	71	53	330
11	Canada (10)	12	33	43	39	53	56	67	303
12	Australia (9)	39	33	44	41	28	52	56	293
13	South Africa (23)	35	24	54	46	41	41	33	274
14	The Netherlands (14)	39	31	38	39	28	48	37	260
15	Mexico (15)	11	32	17	40	32	30	35	197
16	Sweden (29)	36	30	37	48	18	12	12	193
17	Hong Kong (28)	23	28	36	36	34	12	9	178
18	New Zealand (37)	12	23	23	29	40	30	17	174
19	Italy (6)	7	12	10	16	25	15	15	100
20	Norway (25)	15	15	22	14	13	8	11	98
21	Chile (46)	14	13	6	24	19	6	13	95
22	Portugal (40)	15	14	12	17	16	8	9	91
23=	Czech Republic (34)	1	11	14	18	11	14	11	81
	Poland (16)	12	13	19	16	11	7	3	81
25	India (21)	6	14	20	9	12	5	8	74

NB: figure in brackets ( ) = ranking by market size 2005. Source: ZenithOptimedia

The Most Awarded Advertisers in The World 1999 – 2005

		Gunn Report Winner Points							
		1999	2000	2001	2002	2003	2004	2005	TOTAL
1	Volkswagen (7)	109	51	54	39	41	57	65	416
2	Nike (7)	36	48	35	54	40	31	23	267
3	Sony (7)	35	22	27	15	38	51	34	222
4	Adidas (5)	7	20	18	9	4	33	47	138
5	Budweiser (6)	13	21	23	21	22	26	7	133
6	Fox (5)	21	22	23	16	20	6	2	110
7	Axe/Lynx (5)	6	12	15	6	22	18	20	99
8	Guinness (4)	11	37	7	14	13	7	5	94
9	Audi (6)	13	21	12	14	10	11	2	83
10=	Ikea (4)	5	4	10	19	20	13	7	78
	Toyota (4)	8	24	3	15	6	14	8	78
12	BMW (5)	3	7	12	14	14	15	11	76
13	McDonald's (5)	10	17	15	8	15	4	5	74
14	Levi's (4)	9	4	4	20	19	6	11	73
15	MTV (3)	6	10	3	7	23	10	8	67
16	Pepsi (6)	12	9	8	8	9	6	14	66
17	Honda (2)	-	-	2	1	3	36	23	65
18	Mercedes-Benz (4)	6	9	15	12	7	5	10	64
19	Coca-Cola (4)	2	5	2	9	12	10	15	55
20	Mini (3)	-	-	-	1	24	17	11	53
21	Heineken (4)	8	8	4	12	12	7	1	52
22	The Economist (4)	4	5	9	11	5	8	9	51
23	Land Rover (2)	2	10	7	15	4	4	3	45
24	Virgin (3)	13	2	2	1	-	9	17	44
25	FedEx (2)	6	1	3	12	5	10	6	43
26=	Miller (2)	23	5	1	1	2	8	1	41
	Renault (2)	14	2	-	1	7	6	11	41
28	Peugeot (2)	1	2	4	1	13	4	11	36
29	Mattel (2)	3	3	2	9	13	2	1	33

NB: figure in brackets ( ) = times in Top 25 table. To be included above, Advertiser has had to be in Top 25 twice or more

The Most Awarded Production Companies in The World 1999 – 2005

		Gunn Report Winner Points							
		1999	2000	2001	2002	2003	2004	2005	TOTAL
1	Gorgeous Enterprises (London)	17	26	18	57	23	38	13	**192**
2	@radical.media (New York, London, Paris, Sydney etc)	16	24	17	32	28	36	2	**179**
3	Partizan/Partizan Midi Minuit (London, NY, Paris etc)	9	26	27	17	23	60	13	**175**
4	Matching Studio (Bangkok)	5	8	16	13	13	33	20	**108**
5	Hungry Man (New York, London)	17	13	12	16	9	21	19	**107**
6	Phenomena (Bangkok)	1	1	7	8	25	22	39	**103**
7	MJZ (Los Angeles)	6	2	8	4	43	11	19	**93**
8	Garcia Bross (Mexico City)	3	10	10	23	18	12	14	**90**
9	Spectre/Large (London)	2	3	11	18	24	5	22	**85**
10=	Academy (London)	11	19	9	9	13	1	6	**68**
	The Film Factory (Hong Kong, Bangkok)	7	20	13	11	9	4	4	**68**
12	Propaganda/Satellite (New York, London, Hollywood)	9	23	16	13	-	1	-	**62**
13	Czar (Amsterdam & Brussels)	6	11	1	6	13	13	9	**59**
14	Anonymous Content (Culver City)	-	-	1	24	20	9	1	**55**
15=	Outsider (London)	5	12	3	11	10	6	3	**50**
	Stink (London)	-	2	4	11	5	13	15	**50**
17	Biscuit Filmworks (Los Angeles)	-	-	-	2	9	14	23	**48**
18	harvest Films (Santa Monica)	-	-	-	14	15	11	5	**45**
19=	Harry Nash (London)	-	8	23	5	7	1	-	**44**
	Pytka (Venice, CA)	3	12	6	12	6	4	1	**44**
21	Tohokushinsha Film Corp (Tokyo)	-	2	14	7	2	7	10	**42**
22	RSA (Los Angeles, New York, London)	1	7	7	2	16	3	4	**40**
23=	Avion (Toronto)	2	-	3	7	12	13	2	**39**
	Dentsu Tec (Tokyo & Osaka)	1	12	6	11	2	-	7	**39**
	Zero Filmes (Sao Paulo)	1	2	14	5	7	6	4	**39**

The Most Awarded Directors in The World 1999 - 2005

		Gunn Report Winner Points							
		1999	2000	2001	2002	2003	2004	2005	TOTAL
1	Frank Budgen (Great Britain)	16	19	7	44	18	21	8	133
2=	Suthon Petchsuwan (Thailand)	5	5	16	12	12	33	19	102
	Thanonchai Sornsrivichai (Thailand)	1	2	7	8	25	22	37	102
4	Traktor (USA & Sweden)	4	22	26	9	9	21	6	97
5	Daniel Kleinman (Great Britain)	2	3	11	19	25	5	19	84
6	Simon Bross (Mexico)	3	9	9	19	17	7	14	78
7	Baker Smith (USA)	4	2	3	19	19	11	4	62
8	Fredrik Bond (Great Britain & Sweden)	3	9	21	5	12	6	3	59
9	Noam Murro (USA)	6	1	4	2	11	10	22	56
10	Jonathan Glazer (Great Britain)	9	15	6	8	10	1	-	49
11=	Joe Pytka (USA)	3	12	6	12	6	4	1	44
	Ivan Zacharias (Czech Republic & GB)	-	4	4	8	6	11	11	44
13	Bryan Buckley (USA)	1	7	7	10	2	5	10	42
14	Chris Palmer (Great Britain)	3	8	10	6	1	8	5	41
15	Frank Todaro (USA)	3	18	1	6	3	8	1	40
16	Rocky Morton (USA)	6	2	9	3	16	1	2	39
17-	Sergio Amon (Brazil)	1	2	13	5	6	6	4	37
	Matthijs Van Heijningen (The Netherlands)	2	8	4	5	14	2	2	37
19	Lance Acord (USA)	-	-	-	1	7	10	18	36
20=	Diego Kaplan (Argentina & USA)	-	-	-	6	17	7	5	35
	Kuntz & McGuire (USA)	-	1	17	8	7	-	2	35
	Louis Ng (Hong Kong)	7	10	6	6	4	1	1	35
23	Martin Granger (Canada)	-	-	-	6	12	12	4	34
24	Andy Fogwill (Argentina)	1	-	2	3	5	7	10	28
25	Tim Godsall (Canada)	-	-	-	-	8	4	15	27

The Most Awarded Agencies in The World 1999 - 2005

		Gunn Report Winner Points							
		1999	2000	2001	2002	2003	2004	2005	TOTAL
1=	DDB (London)	67	15	26	25	15	31	27	206
	Dentsu (Tokyo & Osaka)	27	31	37	30	25	27	29	206
3	Wieden+Kennedy (Portland, OR & New York)	32	45	7	40	41	14	11	190
4	Abbott Mead Vickers.BBDO (London)	35	47	20	27	21	10	16	176
5	AlmapBBDO (Sao Paulo)	21	28	17	14	15	36	34	165
6	Lowe (London)	27	29	21	23	16	14	20	150
7	Crispin Porter & Bogusky (Miami)	4	14	13	9	50	33	26	149
8=	Bartle Bogle Hegarty (London)	20	15	17	28	27	11	19	137
	TBWA\Paris (Paris)	3	7	13	8	45	28	33	137
10=	Arnold Worldwide (Boston)	25	14	24	14	29	20	10	136
	TBWA\London (London)	38	10	19	7	27	19	16	136
12	Fallon (Minneapolis, MN & New York)	18	43	11	10	18	10	17	127
13	Saatchi & Saatchi (London)	18	22	23	31	12	8	10	124
14	TBWA\Chiat\Day (USA)	8	6	17	22	23	26	21	123
15	Cliff Freeman & Partners (New York)	49	15	25	8	1	5	1	104
16	BBDO (Bangkok)	14	11	15	19	6	21	15	101
17	DDB (Sao Paulo)	24	16	16	11	7	9	11	94
18	DDB (Madrid & Barcelona)	11	19	18	15	8	12	9	92
19=	DDB (USA)	6	18	15	13	10	20	9	91
	Goodby Silverstein & Ptnrs (San Francisco)	20	15	21	2	13	7	13	91
21	Springer & Jacoby (Hamburg)	13	10	16	18	11	2	17	87
22	F/Nazca Saatchi & Saatchi (Sao Paulo)	0	15	20	12	14	6	9	84
23	TBWA Hunt Lascaris (Johannesburg)	11	16	14	16	9	7	8	81
24	Lowe A&B (Buenos Aires)	22	4	10	19	11	5	9	80
25	CraveroLanis Euro RSCG (Buenos Aires)	10	17	22	14	3	8	5	79

The Most Awarded Agencies in The World 1999 - 2005

		Gunn Report Winner Points						
		1999	2000	2001	2002	2003	2004	2005	TOTAL
26	Ogilvy & Mather (Singapore)	14	6	19	7	5	15	12	78
27	BETC Euro RSCG (Paris)	12	5	6	7	11	13	17	71
28=	BBDO (New York)	7	5	8	19	11	9	11	70
	Hakuhodo (Tokyo)	7	14	13	13	9	5	9	70
	Leo Burnett (London)	3	12	31	11	9	-	4	70
31=	DDB (Toronto & Vancouver)	7	9	8	7	13	11	14	69
	Wieden+Kennedy (London)	-	-	1	5	5	35	23	69
33	Del Campo Nazca Saatchi & Saatchi (Buenos Aires)	-	-	1	9	25	9	24	68
34	Jung Von Matt (Hamburg & Munich)	9	10	9	10	3	16	10	67
35	Scholz & Friends (Berlin & Hamburg)	8	5	14	13	4	10	10	64
36=	Forsman & Bodenfors (Gothenburg)	14	8	8	18	8	4	3	63
	Mother (London)	3	2	19	15	4	8	12	63
	Saatchi & Saatchi (Wellington & Auckland)	9	14	13	5	11	5	6	63
39=	BDDP et Fils (Boulogne-Billancourt)	3	10	8	10	13	13	4	61
	CLM/BBDO (Paris)	12	9	18	5	5	8	4	61
41	Saatchi & Saatchi (Singapore)	21	15	5	8	2	5	4	60
42	VegaOlmosPonce (Buenos Aires)	4	8	12	3	15	8	8	58
43	DDB (Paris)	8	11	6	6	3	9	14	57
44	180 Amsterdam (Amsterdam)	-	3	12	1	1	17	22	56
45	Ogilvy & Mather (Bangkok)	10	-	16	7	4	7	11	55
46	Young & Rubicam (Buenos Aires)	7	8	14	7	4	3	11	54
47	Leo Burnett (Chicago)	2	6	3	6	9	15	10	51
48=	Colenso BBDO (Auckland)	-	3	5	11	14	10	7	50
	McCann-Erickson (Madrid)	5	5	8	14	7	11	-	50
50=	Leo Burnett (Prague)	-	2	4	14	10	8	9	47
	Saatchi & Saatchi (Bangkok)	-	-	-	4	13	13	17	47

The Most Awarded Agency Networks in The World 1999 - 2005

		Gunn Report Winner Points							
		1999	2000	2001	2002	2003	2004	2005	TOTAL
1	BBDO Worldwide	135	135	126	144	135	155	153	983
2	DDB Worldwide	148	108	118	126	107	163	134	904
3	TBWA Worldwide	91	85	94	97	129	159	160	815
4	Saatchi & Saatchi	79	85	96	127	110	78	108	683
5	Leo Burnett	58	85	130	95	90	74	81	613
6	Lowe	67	63	74	80	77	62	59	482
7	Ogilvy & Mather	56	52	88	65	51	87	70	469
8	Wieden+Kennedy	39	46	9	54	53	62	34	297
9	Young & Rubicam	47	36	48	67	32	24	28	282
10	Euro RSCG	21	37	47	26	33	48	55	267
11	JWT	15	16	31	28	51	60	52	253
12	McCann-Erickson	16	29	37	47	42	36	23	230
13	Dentsu	33	31	38	35	26	31	30	224
14	Arnold Worldwide	30	21	33	23	35	29	14	185
15	Bartle Bogle Hegarty	20	15	17	35	46	20	24	177
16	FCB	36	24	21	25	28	15	27	176
17	Fallon	18	47	18	14	30	18	22	167
18	Publicis	16	18	15	15	11	26	24	125
19	Grey	19	20	16	12	13	14	9	103
20	Springer & Jacoby	13	10	16	18	13	2	18	90

The Gunn Report Winners Each Year 1999-2005 Summary

The Most Awarded TV Commercials & Campaigns in The World — Ad Pts

Year		Country	Ad Pts
1999	OUTPOST.COM • Band / Forehead / Cannon	USA	25
2000	GUINNESS • Surfer	Great Britain	25
2001	FOX SPORTS TV/NBA • Alan & Jerome campaign	USA	20
2002	REEBOK • Sofa	Great Britain	23
2003	PEUGEOT 206 • The Sculptor	Italy	22
2004	HONDA ACCORD • Cog	Great Britain	38
2005	HONDA DIESEL • Grrr	Great Britain	35

The Most Awarded Print Ads & Campaigns in The World — Ad Pts

Year		Country	Ad Pts
1999	VOLKSWAGEN/AFFORDABILITY • Wedding	Great Britain	26
2000	VIRGINIA HOLOCAUST MUSEUM • campaign	USA	14
2001	VOLKSWAGEN OF AMERICA • Hey, there's a... campaign	USA	17
2002	CLUB 18-30 HOLIDAYS • Bar / Beach / Pool	Great Britain	27
2003	LEVI'S CLASSIC MEN'S 501's • Hugging & campaign	Singapore	16
2004	VOLKSWAGEN POLO • Cops	Great Britain	25
2005	TAMIYA MODEL KITS SHOP • Light Bulb / Frog / Watermelon	Thailand	20

The Most Awarded Countries in The World — Winner Pts

Year		Winner Pts
1999	USA	298
2000	USA	306
2001	USA	250
2002	USA	250
2003	USA	299
2004	USA	234
2005	USA	196

The Most Awarded Advertisers in The World — Winner Pts

Year		Winner Pts
1999	Volkswagen	109
2000	Volkswagen	51
2001	Volkswagen	54
2002	Nike	54
2003	Volkswagen	41
2004	Volkswagen	57
2005	Volkswagen	65

The Gunn Report Winners Each Year 1999-2005 Summary

The Most Awarded Production Companies in The World

		Winner Pts
1999	Gorgeous Enterprises (London) / Hungry Man (New York & Santa Monica)	1st= 17
2000	Gorgeous Enterprises (London)	26
2001	Partizan (New York & London)	26
2002	Gorgeous Enterprises (London)	57
2003	Morton Jankel Zander (Los Angeles)	43
2004	Partizan (London, Los Angeles, Paris)	60
2005	Phenomena (Bangkok)	39

The Most Awarded Directors in The World

		Winner Pts
1999	Frank Budgen (Great Britain)	16
2000	Traktor (USA & Sweden)	22
2001	Traktor (USA & Sweden)	26
2002	Frank Budgen (Great Britain)	44
2003	Daniel Kleinman (Great Britain) / Thanonchai Sornsrivichai (Thailand)	1st= 25
2004	Suthon Petchsuwan (Thailand)	33
2005	Thanonchai Sornsrivichai (Thailand)	37

The Most Awarded Advertising Agencies in The World

		Winner Pts
1999	BMP DDB (London)	67
2000	Abbott Mead Vickers.BBDO (London)	47
2001	Dentsu (Tokyo & Osaka)	37
2002	Wieden+Kennedy (Portland, OR)	40
2003	Crispin Porter & Bogusky (Miami)	50
2004	AlmapBBDO (Sao Paulo)	36
2005	AlmapBBDO (Sao Paulo)	34

The Most Awarded Agency Networks in The World

		Winner Pts
1999	DDB Worldwide	148
2000	BBDO Worldwide	135
2001	Leo Burnett	130
2002	BBDO Worldwide	144
2003	BBDO Worldwide	135
2004	DDB Worldwide	163
2005	TBWA Worldwide	160

Contents